LOST NEW YORK

W9-BNF-722

NATHAN SILVER

LOST
YO

NEW
YORK

EXPANDED AND UPDATED

A MARINER BOOK

HOUGHTON MIFFLIN COMPANY

BOSTON / NEW YORK

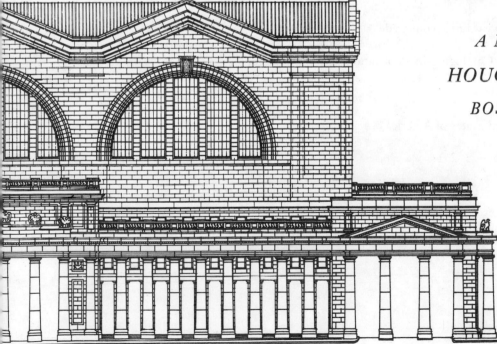

For information about permission to reproduce selections from this book,
write to Permissions, Houghton Mifflin Company, 215 Park Avenue South,
New York, New York 10003.

Visit our Web site: www.hmco.com/trade.

Library of Congress Cataloging-in-Publication data is available.

ISBN 0-618-05475-8

Printed in the United States of America

CRW 10 9 8 7 6 5 4 3 2 1

ACKNOWLEDGMENTS, 1966.   This book would never have been begun if the funds for the original exhibit had not been made available by the Columbia University School of Architecture. Gratitude is particularly due to David E. Glasser, Raymond Lifchez, and Dean Kenneth A. Smith. While I was seeking photographs in archives and picture collections, the following people were most helpful: Adolph K. Placzek, Librarian of the Avery Architectural Library at Columbia; Hedy Backlin of the Cooper Union Museum; James J. Heslin of the New-York Historical Society; Romana Javitz, Curator of the Picture Collection, New York Public Library; Vivian Hibbs of the Metropolitan Museum of Art; Henriette Beal and Albert K. Baragwanath of the Museum of the City of New York. Others who helped me were Margot Gayle and Mrs. J. DeW. Peltz of the Metropolitan Opera Association. For dates and other historical information, I relied on several pioneer works, particularly those of I. N. Phelps Stokes and John A. Kouwenhoven. Many photographs were taken by just a few photographers whose interest and devotion in recording old New York buildings made their recollection possible. Among them were the Wurts brothers, the Byrons, H. N. Tiemann, Berenice Abbott and Samuel Gottscho. Their work has my greatest esteem and appreciation. Some of those who offered advice, information and help during the writing of the text were Professor James G. Van Derpool and Alan Burnham of the Landmarks Preservation Commission; Henry Hope Reed, Jr., of the Municipal Art Society; Stephen Zoll; and William Blackburn. Betsy Smith patiently answered many questions about typography and layout. Commissioner Evelyn Haynes and Mrs. Regina Kellerman of the Landmarks Preservation Commission and Mr. Baragwanath read the text, generously sharing their expert knowledge of New York. Joyce Hartman of Houghton Mifflin not only edited but in some ways masterminded the book. None of these people are responsible for my judgment and errors.

ACKNOWLEDGMENTS, 2000.   I'm delighted to record further gratitude to numerous people — journalists, architects, municipal historians, friends and relatives. My particular great thanks to Edwin Hemsley; Christopher Gray and his Office for Metropolitan History; Glenn Young and his scholars at Applause Theatre & Cinema Books; Mark Read; Dee Wells; Jade Charnin; my brother Robert Silver of Schwartz/Silver Architects; Benny Nash; Chairman Louis Auchincloss and Anne Easterling of the Museum of the City of New York; the late James Marston Fitch; Laura Rosen of MTA Bridges and Tunnels; Angela Troisi of the New York *Daily News*; Valerie Zars of the Liaison Agency; and my new editor extraordinary, Susan Canavan at Houghton Mifflin. Recent written materials that lightened my task include the invaluable *Encyclopedia of New York City* and the four times invaluable *New York 1880, 1900, 1930, 1960*, plus the architectural discernment of the *New York Times*'s House & Home editor Linda Lee and Christopher Gray's "Streetscapes" documentary features (so good I name him twice), and *The New Yorker*'s present and former writers of the architectural column "The Sky Line," Paul Goldberger and the late, sadly missed Brendan Gill. (A negative acknowledgment to the New York Yacht Club, which denied my request for a photo of the America's Cup trophy on display before it was lost in 1983 — and so far, one notes, they haven't won it back.) My book title begot a cavalcade of titular Losts, and I learned from some of them. At first suspicious and slightly resentful of other LNYs that I stumbled across, I enjoyed an interactive-fiction computer game called Lost New York, and picked up a bit from a *Time Out* cover story entitled "Lost New York" that cheekily used a cover shot of Pennsylvania Station's glazed train shed not unlike my own original cover. Bless you all anyway.

— *N. S.*

To my father, who grew up on Broome Street

And my mother, who met him uptown

CONTENTS.

PREFACE.

...TO THE FIRST EDITION: This book began as an exhibit at the Columbia University School of Architecture. By 1963 it seemed urgent to make some sort of plea for architectural preservation in New York City. It had been announced that Pennsylvania Station would be razed, a final solution appeared likely for the 39th Street Metropolitan Opera, and the commercial buildings of Worth Street were being pounded into landfill for a parking lot. I suggested that the collective picture of some vanished first-rate architecture would make a sobering reminder of how much finer a city New York could have been with its all-time best buildings still intact. With help from many, the show was planned. We hoped it would be an editorial for preservation, and wanted to support the growing local awareness that some legislative protection was needed for many urban landmarks.

I began to look for photographs of old New York buildings in archives and picture collections. What had seemed at first a relatively simple, closed-end research job proved to be a vast undertaking. Thousands of buildings deserved to have their likenesses rescued from oblivion. Often, ones I thought of showing had only poor photographs available, or none. Some of the buildings were unidentified — with not only their architects unknown, but even their uses and locations in the city obscure. Moreover, it soon became clear that, just as a city is more than a collection of buildings, *Lost New York* had also to take notice of other aspects of life here — the old places of recreation, the working districts, the tenement neighborhoods, transportation systems and parks.

When the exhibit opened in January 1964 it was still a work in progress. Yet the response was stimulating — and the remarks rather unexpected. The typical comment (mostly from architects and their families, at that) was not "Too bad this was lost, it was beautiful," but much more often "Too bad this was lost, it was old." The commonest assumption was that I was arguing the justice and worthiness of preservation *for the sake of the past*. Yet there was some confusion somewhere, because the typical landmark-preservation response to a need for the past had been to call for legislation to save the few monuments that matter. For example, in an article called "Preservation" in the October 1965 *Journal of the Society of Architectural Historians*, Alan Gowans said: "Almost any building has historical associations for somebody; almost any building manifests some style; almost any building is a delight in somebody's eyes. The result is that, generally speaking, whenever any old building is threatened with destruction, for whatever reason, there is always somebody ready to defend it . . . The only effect of operating on principles that justify saving everything is to make 'preservationist' a synonym for 'obstructionist' in the minds of developers and planners."

But this attitude would stop discussion just where it should start. *Why* is someone always ready to defend an old building? All we have to account for it is that unsatisfactory word "nostalgia" — psychologically a probably very interesting concept. It seems to me unconscientious to disparage its basis. That is why this book has gone on from the Columbia exhibit.

Now, after a far broader search into New York's past, I believe that while *preservationism* may have as its objective "the survival of the fittest" (Gowans), that leaves aside why some things in the history of art or culture that are not terribly fit should still be maintained. I challenge the adequacy of Gowans's assertion that "the basic question to ask in deciding on preservation is not what visual pleasure and intellectual significance given buildings have for us, but what they had for the generation that built them." If that's as relevant to our needs as architectural historians are prepared to get, we're defenseless. *Conservationism* must also be our concern, with the responsibility shared by ordinary people. If architecture is somewhat the art of beautiful buildings but fundamentally the art of human use (as I believe), then conservation of good use is a matter of concern for everyone, and conservation is not "obstructionist" but wise. That is the point of this book, and the aspect of *Lost New York* best remembered.

...TO THE EXPANDED EDITION: If my last paragraph above seems rather obvious and incontrovertible now, it's because few can still remember that in 1966 when it was written, conservation was a word seldom used in relation to architectural or cultural maintenance. (In those antediluvian days we conserved only threatened animals and plants.) It's wonderful to have reached a golden age when one is no longer fearful about obstructing destructive planners and developers.

That applies as well to my own age. When I first completed *Lost New York* I was a twenty-seven-year-old assistant professor of architecture at Columbia. I revised it as a sixty-three year-old retired head of a school of architecture who has lived more than half his life in another country. I now register New York's changed cityscapes as much through my reception of others' words and attitudes as through my earlier personal experiences. My subject has become for me less a chronicle of yesterday, more a memorious vision that I see before me now. I suspect this is true for many unrelocated New Yorkers as well. In this expanded edition, I've therefore tried to account for a discontinuously engaged though more complicated response to the city. A few mistakes have been corrected. A new section called "Places and Moments" is about metropolitan epiphanies that occurred at lost New York scenes, with some "moments" that I remember and some that I feel deserve memorializing. Another new section is a re-registration of some subjects that were previously listed under "Landmarks in Danger" and are now among the vanished, with additions. It is called "In Memoriam," though "New Lost City Ramblers," another title that came to me, might have been as appropriate for reclassified lost buildings as for an old band on Smithsonian Folkways (the Smithsonian regrettably doesn't do disks of lost buildings). I've deleted the "Landmarks in Danger" section otherwise, since it now feels safe to skew my account more straightforwardly toward memory.

Rather than depend on a mere book to point the crabby finger, perhaps New York should celebrate its now wider perception of conservation by taking up a public collection to build a Temple of Metropolitan Unworthies, on the model of the Temple of British Worthies at Stowe — a place to brood over the villains of lost New York. There don't need to be many busts, and we ought to show optimism by leaving only a few empty niches. Most perpetrators of destruction, after all, are unknowing or simply ignorant. I would personally nominate only three Unworthies to remember with disdain: A. J. Greenough, the President of the Pennsylvania Railroad Company in the early 1960s, who wantonly engineered the destruction of Pennsylvania Station to improve his company's balance sheet; Anthony Bliss, the President of the Metropolitan Opera Company in the late 1960s, who helped finance the company's move to Lincoln Center with a contract that ensured smithereens for the old building; and Robert Moses, Commissioner Plenipotentiary and Rubblemaker General, for his recurrent terminations of any place he autonomously decided upon. Greenough, Moses and Bliss. (Remember them with a hiss!) Their self-satisfied visages wouldn't be a pretty sight, but if they are remembered for what they destroyed it should be a good place to begin.

London, January 2000

LOST NEW YORK

... I am with you, you men and women of a generation, or ever so many
        generations hence. ...
What is it then between us?
What is the count of the scores or hundreds of years between us?

... I too lived, Brooklyn of ample hills was mine,
I too walk'd the streets of Manhattan island, and bathed in the waters
        around it,
I too felt the curious abrupt questionings stir within me.

      – Walt Whitman, *Crossing Brooklyn Ferry*

The business lunch took place at the Plaza, an excellent first-class hotel
of the old type. I like those vast and handsome hotels which are not at all
in modern style but which have acquired a past through their richness and
substantiality. There are living pasts and dead pasts. Some pasts are the
liveliest instigators of the present and the best springboards into the future ...

      – Le Corbusier, *When the Cathedrals Were White*

Introduction
1966
    Cities reveal as much about time as about place. They usually start from small settlements which grow
and change at first in a direct response to site conditions, climate, and available materials. This corre-
sponds to the fundamental task of architecture — to protect man from the tyranny of nature. As a
settlement becomes better established, building typically turns to the development of institutions. An
orderly pattern for these is the second great task of architecture, and once a settlement has reached this
point, it can no longer be called a primitive or pioneer place. The settlement, growing and changing,
next takes up forms that clarify the livelihood, culture, and communications of the inhabitants, and meet

1

the needs of an expanding population. Urban geographers can look at plans of such human settlements and determine many facts about the people who live in them. The question of what they are seems to have something to do with how long they have been in one place.

If a settlement is left to change as it will, the ever more complex requirements of life soon make it lose its initial clarity. In modern cities, the many paths and purposes of the inhabitants eventually generate subtle and non-architectural facilities (the conference room instead of the meeting hall; the telephone instead of the market square). The city then becomes free to adapt itself to ephemera, and most have done so. The pervasive sights of most cities at present are stoplights, billboards, parking lots, unrelated shopfronts. Some urban theorists, such as Kevin Lynch, have argued for a return to the "imageability" of the city when its paths and purposes were simple. Others, such as Jane Jacobs and Herbert Gans, have maintained that modern life is too complex for planned clarity in cities to be desirable or even possible.

Quite outside the thesis and antithesis of this debate, something recognized by all parties is how satisfying old buildings can be. When seen in the context of growth and change, there is no mystery about why this should be so. An old building is usually one that has continued to make sense in its relationship with both its place and its users. The building's survival through time — this *alone* — is a circumstantially strong indication of its value. If time is a dimension that clarifies and enriches things, the conservation of such buildings would seem worthwhile.

To provide a basis for opinion about the buildings shown in this book, some notes on architectural survival seem appropriate. In the case of New York (as of any city), history provides strong indications of what is likely to be useful and meaningful. The notes therefore start with characteristics of New York's essential formation, including the peculiar New York qualities of common experience. Then they go on to the significance of the past for its own sake, and forces and proposals that naturally operate for change. They conclude with present municipal powers with respect to architectural continuity, and prospects for the future. This is all meant to provide a dialectic for discussion about the vanished architecture shown here, and how it was most valuable. But it is also hoped that these notes will suggest some logical ways of reappraising the need for continuity in the urban environment.

I. The colony is now established on the Manhates, where a fort has been staked out by Master Kryn Fredrycks, an engineer. It is planned to be of large dimensions . . . The counting-house there is kept in a stone building thatched with reed; the other houses are of the bark of trees. Each has his own house. The Director and commercial agent live together. There are thirty ordinary houses on the east side of the river, which runs nearly north and south . . .

François Molemaecker is busy building a horse-mill over which shall be constructed a spacious room sufficient to accommodate a large congregation, and then a tower is to be erected where the bells brought from Porto Rico will be hung . . . The houses of the Hollanders now stand outside the fort, but when that is completed they will all repair within, so as to garrison it and be secure from sudden attack . . .

2

When the fort, staked out at the Manhates, will be completed, it is to be named Amsterdam.*

The choice of New York was an accident of water. Its geography provided a harbor and afforded natural positions of defense both at the passage of the Narrows from the lower bay and at the Hudson estuary. Although one of Europe's "most memorable occurrences," the settlement of New Amsterdam was done in a matter-of-fact fashion by the West India Company. Manhattan was bought and paid for, buildings were staked out and built. This was all odd to the Indians, who knew nothing of ownership of the land. They had sold the right to inhabit it, to hunt and fish and cultivate the soil. They themselves would have moved on in case of drought or bad hunting. The Europeans brought to the New World their own ideas about possession and property, their assumption being that building was more significant than land. The most important aspect of the new settlement therefore emerged at the very start, when the new occupants showed that possession of the land meant permanent ownership and that the new community was to be there to stay.

Manhattan soon had many settlements on it which slowly grew together: the Bowery, Sappohanican (later Greenwich Village), Harlem, Manhattanville, Bloomingdale, and Inwood. These were villages, rural agricultural centers scattered over the island, connected to the separate small town of New Amsterdam at the southern tip. According to a plan of 1660, New Amsterdam itself had only about 300 houses, which stopped at Wall Street. Streets divided the town into about twenty blocks. The shape of the town layout was related to three main features: to Fort Amsterdam, a palisaded fort south of the present Bowling Green with four salient points; to the Heerewegh (later Broadway), which ran north; and to a canal where Broad Street is now.

First growth By 1670, six years after the English had captured the town, a boat basin had been constructed on the East River side, a market had been built on piles over the water, and a slaughterhouse constructed outside the town wall. In 1696 the first Trinity Church was built. The tower of Trinity and the polygonal cupola of the first city hall were New York's most outstanding landmarks. Stepped-gable buildings were giving way mostly to timber adaptations of English houses. About the same time, walls of many of the stone houses began to be marked with iron date numerals in consciousness of age.

The Manhattan settlement had been set up by the Dutch to serve as a trading center, and trade remained its fundamental purpose through the English colonial period. An act of 1680 gave New York millers the sole right throughout the province to grind and bolt flour. Prosperity grew so greatly as a result of this law that, while it was only in effect for fourteen years, the population of the town tripled and the number of buildings and city revenues more than doubled during that time.

By the middle of the 18th century the old wall at Wall Street was down, streets beyond were being routinely added by survey, and landfill operations were taking place around the perimeter of the island. The meeting of the Stamp Act Congress in New York in 1765 demonstrated that the city had become not only a trade center, but an important political center of the colonies as well. After the Revolution it became the first federal capital. When Alexander Hamilton became Washington's Secretary of the

---

* From *Historical Narrative of All the Most Memorable Occurrences Which Have Come to Pass in Europe*, an account by Nicolaes van Wassenaer, published in Holland in 1626. This translation is from *Mirror for Gotham* by Bayrd Still, N.Y.U. Press, 1956.

Treasury, his Bank of New York was a means and part of the plan to put the country on a firm postwar financial basis. New York's financial leadership was to remain pre-eminent among American cities.

After the Revolution a kind of monumental architecture was regularly appearing. Some important commissions given to Pierre Charles L'Enfant also signaled a change to French-oriented taste in building (see page 90), just as there had been a change from Dutch to English style almost 100 years earlier. Vernacular construction remained about the same: mostly timber buildings, with stone and brick construction largely downtown and for wealthier people.

The growth of the city and increasing value of downtown land required the building-over of natural land features. The Collect Pond, a fresh water lake north of what is now Foley Square, was filled in 1803; a few years later the hills that had made it a basin were leveled. The Mangin-McComb City Hall, New York's architectural masterpiece, was incompleted but in use in 1811. From it issued the Commissioners' Plan, a map eight feet long which plotted future streets up to 155th. It showed an absolutely geometrical gridiron of rectangles (except for Broadway, too familiar to be changed). Nothing like Central Park was proposed, but small park-squares four blocks long were staggered at about twenty-block intervals. The rectangular geometry was familiar. Such patterns in towns had been built as early as the 5th century B.C., and they had straightforward advantages: good economies of usable land due to the conventions of rectangular building; convenient location-finding with only two directional "fixes," the minimum requirement; a simple traffic situation on the streets at each intersection (at least for travel at the speed of horses; T-shaped intersections would have been more suitable for faster vehicular traffic).

Planned growth

It is probable that aesthetic considerations, apart from those related to economy and hygiene, carried little weight with the New York commissioners. In this they were not different from planners of the Renaissance, who, according to Siegfried Giedion, were also disinterested in the unity of the straight avenues they built.* But it would be unfair to condemn gridiron plans as lacking possibilities. The design principle of the street in perspective has found an effective response on many streets in New York where cornice heights and building facades are coordinated. (The English planner Lord Llewellyn-Davies has called these facades on linear streets New York's "endless architecture.") On the other hand, a linear street can have a section-by-section series of relationships structured by the street, like individual beads on a chain. There is more of this kind of diversity, charm and sensibility on 55th Street, for example, than in many medieval towns.

However, the main problem of gridiron plans is that they are unrelated to the natural terrain, and with their dogmatic patterns tend to obliterate land features. In New York, the Commissioners' Plan of 1811 must bear full responsibility for this. Only the fact that the planners anticipated nothing but garden suburbs for the endless blocks helps explain a design which prophesied (and has become in some parts of New York) a frighteningly monotonous sea of city.

New York building is not only a question of *why*, but *how*. The kind of construction, the building-plan types in commonplace use, the notions about spaces inside, the decoration favored — these are all building characteristics, and in the texture of the city the slow development and change of building characteristics is the nub. It is also a quality of the city's essential formation, since the productive variety of these forms is an accumulation of single decisions related to many individuals.

Early building

---

* *Space, Time, and Architecture*, Harvard University Press, 1941.

New York's building designs can be most rewardingly studied in the varieties of houses and commercial buildings. It is instructive to look beyond Federal or Greek Revival decoration to the more essential changes which affected the quality of life within. In New York row houses, for example (pages 128–137), there is the relocation of the staircase from the back, where it reduced light and air, to the center of the hall, allowing extra windows for rooms instead of the stair. Or there is the change from pitched roofs with dormer windows to flat roofs with more headroom on the attic floor, which corresponded to the development of satisfactory asphalt and cheap metal roofing techniques.

From the 1830s on, many of the lofts put up for warehousing and the textile trades were miracles of refinement, lightness, economy and grace. There was nothing like them elsewhere in America (not until later). Prefabricated specimens were even sent abroad in the 1850s. If anything should forever stand as a radiant image of the essential New York, it ought to be the commercial buildings — the ones built on straightforward systems of bays with iron ties, the cast iron fronts, the wide open glass walls, the primitive lifts improving in design as loft succeeded loft — the Eccentric Mill Works, Harper's, Stewart's (pages 166–168). The uniqueness and significance of these buildings and the historical development of the light industrial type mark their participation in the city's early growth. Later types of building, the skyscraper for example, found their highest expression elsewhere, even if New York built the most. But the best and purest that New York can offer are the commercial buildings which were formed as a perfect response to contemporary needs, in that hour of inspired invention.

The first park Though small squares were shown in the 1811 Commissioners' Plan, parklands were left out. They cost money, were associated with private gardens of the European aristocracy, and interfered with land speculation (they were also called potential nests for criminals). Since all these things were true, the advocates of Central Park had to overcome many such objections before coming to terms with the natural one: the fact that the selected site was a wasteland. The park squares of London were often groves and gardens preserved intact from noble estates, but there was no equivalent site preparation in the case of New York. Until the 1850s, the city was built only up to about 42nd Street. In 1850, the area from 59th to 110th Streets and Fifth to Eighth Avenues contained scrubland, farms, squatters' shacks, and reservoirs for Croton aqueduct water. The decision to build a great park there was partly aided by the availability of relief workers in the 1857 Depression, although that came after construction of the park was under way. The magnitude of the project was undoubtedly more an expression of the linear nature of New York's growth, led on by the cheapness of land to the north.

Frederick Law Olmsted's park is twice as large as Regent's Park or Hyde Park in London, and only Dublin, Vienna and Paris have bigger ones. In its landscape design, it is all that Humphry Repton ever proposed for an English country estate. There was even a sheep meadow, like the working pastureland within English estate gardens. As it came to be built, the basic New York topography of outcropped rock still shows through, but such ancient configurations as McGown's Pass of Revolutionary War fame were swept away. The construction of the park cost $16,500,000, a vast sum at the time even for so vast an undertaking.

The design was remarkably beautiful and remarkably artificial, in the sense quoted by Repton from Burke: "No work of art can be great but as it deceives. To be otherwise is the prerogative of nature only." Central Park's richness and variety should be understood as essentially an artistic and artificial effort, in order to appreciate the delicate balance of elements that was established between wild and controlled parts, open vistas and densely planted sections. The growing up of the city around the park in later days has therefore enhanced rather than detracted from the magical artifice of the design. The greens and copses with the city skyline beyond make the park effectively a middle-distance phenomenon, allowing no chance of mistaking its perfect form as mere countryside. The backdrop of buildings also makes the enormous two-and-a-half by a half mile size of the park visually clear and understandable in terms of human scale. 150,000 people can be within it on a pleasant summer day, but the park is artistically a miniature for all of that — a tiny image of nature. Its original layout has been seriously compromised quite recently (see page 39), but Central Park remains the greatest example anywhere of English landscape design, a major art, and the most essential of the fundamental elements of the city.

The passage of time has made more emphatic most of the early tendencies of New York's foundation period. The city became the financial and managerial headquarters of the country, and, as the principal American port, the immigration center. Many of the immigrants stayed and provided cheap labor for a generation, supplying industries with workers while bankers offered risk capital. New York's garment industry is one of the permanent survivors of this period, and the mechanics of the situation still work today.

Emerging characteristics

New York was not only closest to Europe by being a great port, it also tended eastward by sharing some European manners and European social divisions. Henry James called the first Waldorf-Astoria the "characteristic" of the city, though the characteristic in 1904 might more easily have been the poverty and misery and crime that Jacob Riis reported. As a cosmopolitan community, however, New York took on the social and cultural eminence of a European capital, eliminating Boston and Philadelphia from contention by the end of the 19th century. The lack of a national political center in the country's largest city only underlined New York's preoccupations as clearly differentiated from those of the American heartland.

Financial and cultural forces acted together to form the theater and film industries that were based in New York, and these eventually helped provide the liberal backing and audience that encouraged writers and painters and dancers to live and work there. After World War II, the permanent location of the United Nations began to give the New York international life some focus, and perhaps at last the Waldorf-Astoria (the new one, this time), with its residence of the U.S. Ambassador to the U.N., became a New York "characteristic."

The experience of New York

New York's essential formation is only part of what is unique about the city. If what matters can be measured by common experience, there are familiar attitudes toward some of the physical realities of New York that can be read as clues. These are ordinary things, real or imagined, that are "known" — a sort of city psychology, a New York *thing*. The architect Louis Sullivan (in his 1901 book *Kindergarten Chats*) knew that New York had a characteristic mentality that was very different from that of Chicago.

One of the more immediately sensed aspects of New York is its economic richness and fatness — the dignity of capitalism, often expressed in architecture. This was as essential an ingredient of Pennsylvania Station (page 32) as it is of the new Chase Manhattan building. Both these places seem to ring true for New York, because the spirit of the city is within them.

The garment industry and the buildings that housed it are also places clearly expressing New York things, as are the downtown canyons between skyscrapers, and also the districts for amusement, from the Tenderloin of old days to the present theater-lined 45th Street. Then there is the current equivalent of vernacular building: the aluminum and porcelain store fronts, the Coca-Cola ads over delicatessens, the new aluminum double-hung sash in tenement windows. This much is ephemeral, but it ranges over to absolutely essential characteristics such as the brick and the brownstone, the sheet metal cornices and cast-iron railings of row houses, the old granite curbstones and block street paving, the vanishing shepherd's crook lampposts.

All the commonplace, prevalent building materials and familiar methods and practices contribute to the urban fabric and the experience of New York things. Every detail matters. It is important to perceive that hardware stores are often painted orange out front, and that the color of newspaper kiosks and shoeshine stands is green.

Some of the *imagined* things about New York are also fundamental and important. The fact that it is "a melting pot," for example; the fact that the sidewalks are "paved with gold." Horace Greeley must be remembered (he reputedly said go West, but he stayed in New York); and the heroes of Paul Goodman's *Empire City* and Nathaniel West's *Miss Lonelyhearts*. Also Alfred Kazin as *A Walker in the City;* and O. Henry, Edith Wharton, F. Scott Fitzgerald and the Plaza fountain. The ideas of New York that are present here — though some are romantic or largely imaginary — have become part of New York experience, even to distant strangers who have only heard about them.

There are a great number of New York things, "characteristics" in the Henry James sense. Many of them are very vague, special, not perceptible or not common to everyone, but they are still knowable and valuable (though they are emphatically not all *visual* things). The most significant of all New York things may be that there are so many different paths and aspects.

The significance of the past II. Like any place else, New York's essential characteristics are rooted in times past. There appears to be good reason to believe that people take special notice and gain special strength from familiar surroundings. They seem to respond to the past in a somewhat consistent, if uncritical, way.

The smallest elements of the physical world are the first external things important to babies. Data about surroundings is gradually learned, with the first things often remaining the most precious. The child's toys, his bed, the pattern of cracks in the ceiling may be memories that will never leave him. The Dutch architect Aldo van Eyck calls attention to the place of the doorstep in meaning and remembrance. It is physically insignificant, yet it is the link between the hearth and the world. Again and again one crosses it and returns to it.

Movement along familiar streets is accomplished by proceeding from perceptual detail to detail. The most elemental things seem to be recognized first. There are streets that one knows from the slope of the sidewalks, though one can't remember what buildings are there. Memory and familiarity are sequences of trifling impressions, like corners, steps, doorjambs. They constitute the mechanics of experience. Architecture, when it is at its best, arouses the spirit and methodically organizes these impressions.

In addition to normal perception and awareness of surroundings, there are ample grounds to believe that all people are conditioned by certain incunabula of cultural and individual orientation. Sir James Frazer's *The Golden Bough* has explored the myths and superstitions that seem to underlie much of primeval experience. Jungian psychology is concerned with the common symbolic elements of existence. The great landmark ideas of Ernst Cassirer based an entire philosophy on the meaning of signs and symbols, one that has been in the mainstream of thought since about 1925. It is clear that man is not rootless, but has long taps back into time.

People value old things, not just for their rarity as antiques, but for their history of human use. They are moved by the gouges and dents in a library table, the smell of an old pipe, the comfort of old clothes. But not only use is significant — the hidden relationship of things to us is very important. People are fascinated by their own family histories. They will travel thousands of miles to walk the streets where their grandfathers lived. The smallest details of the relevant past are a testament, as Marcel Proust knew. In *Remembrance of Things Past* a man's being is shown by a revelation of his total expenditure of time, explained through the description of vivid scenes at particular places, with full details given. Combray, one of Proust's places — nothing more than a landscape and some familiar things — turns out to have the greatest power to explain and recreate the people who lived there.

In his 1964 book, *The Eternal Present*,* Siegfried Giedion is concerned with questions of the significance of the past to our own period. He finds that it has " . . . become apparent that human life is not limited to a single lifespan but goes far beyond. It is as impossible to sever its contacts with the past as to prevent its contacts with the future. Something lives within us which forms part of the very backbone of human dignity: I call this the demand for continuity."

If continuity is as basic to us as Giedion believes, then there must be more to nostalgia than sentimental longing. We may find within it secrets about who we are and where we came from, last week or a thousand years before. Some of these secrets about our lives are disclosed by every corner of a familiar city, soaked in meaning and memory. But architecture itself is freighted with the greatest temporal meaning. This is because it is *devised* to consolidate the necessities of a time, in a place. John Ruskin, in *The Seven Lamps of Architecture* (1849), gave as a key element of his architectural theory "the lamp of memory."

Architecture depends on development through time in order to be clearly related to society and culture. All that is really meant by a building's "style" is that is it more or less understandable in terms of time. The greatest buildings are practically radioactive with history. Regardless of how old or new they are, they tell a true story of life, since they were devised to serve and symbolize human use. An encounter with magnificent architecture irradiates even someone alienated and disaffected. In *You Can't Go Home Again*,† such is Pennsylvania Station for Thomas Wolfe:

> The station, as he entered it, was murmurous with the immense and distant sound of time. Great, slant beams of moted light fell ponderously athwart the station's floor and the calm voice of time hovered along the walls and ceiling of that mighty room, distilled out of the voices and movements of the people who swarmed beneath. It had the murmur of a distant sea, the languorous lapse and flow of waters on a beach. It was elemental, detached, indifferent to the lives of men. They contributed to it as drops of rain contribute to a river that draws its flood and movement majestically from great depths, out of purple hills at evening.
>
> Few buildings are vast enough to hold the sound of time, and . . . there was a superb fitness in the fact that the one which held it better than all others should be a railroad station. For here, as nowhere else on earth, men were brought together for a moment at the beginning or end of their innumerable journeys, here one saw their greetings and farewells, here, in a single instant, one got the entire picture of human destiny. Men came and went, they passed and vanished, all were moving through the moments of their lives to

* Pantheon Books, Inc.
† Charles Scribner's Sons, 1940.

death, all made small tickings in the sound of time — but the voice of time remained aloof and unperturbed, a drowsy and eternal murmur below the immense and distant roof.

The past is important because a sense of continuity is necessary to people — the knowledge that some things have a longer than mortal existence. Affirmation of this can be sought in nature and art. Cities, as the greatest works of man, provide the deepest assurance that this is so. They do it in individual ways, so as to be meaningful to many, by revealing and asserting the sometimes hidden mysteries of their being. Cities are places where different styles converge and mix. As a cultural manifestation, this may be a city's greatest function — its ability to present the full record of the past. Lewis Mumford put it most succinctly of all: "In the city, time becomes visible."

Forces that alter the city

While cities must adapt if they are to remain responsive to the needs and wishes of their inhabitants, they need not change in a heedless and suicidal fashion. It is therefore worth looking at the way some unplanned forces for change operate, to see whether they sometimes work against the needs and wishes of many citizens.

Repair and neglect

The most common force of change is deterioration and replacement, most frequently when buildings undergo repairs. Some buildings in the world are over a thousand years old, but the elemental construction materials of which they are made — stone and tile and heavy timber — are still in the slow process of deterioration. When deterioration is very marked, it is usually because negligence has allowed necessary repairs to accumulate. Perhaps the building has outlived its usefulness and a completely new building is anticipated. In rental properties — and most of the buildings within American cities are in this category — it might be expedient for an owner to neglect his property, hoping to draw off his rents and sell to someone else before too long. In New York, where patterns of discrimination and some housing shortages still exist, this sort of temporizing quickly leads to conditions of drastic disintegration. Tenants realize that the condition of their lives only affects their landlord in the size of his rent rolls, and therefore have no reason to feel that his house is theirs. Where other forces (such as a scorched-earth planning program) may become operational, the landlord need only wait for his property to be officially called part of a slum, and then reap further rewards when the building is acquired for clearance.

Fashions in land values

Most city buildings are destroyed in order to be replaced by larger buildings. Land values in central city areas are forever on the rise. But land values must be considered not only according to solid worth. There are also matters of social selectivity, prestige, and other things that work according to fashion, and New York has some of the most fashion-conscious real estate in the world. In 1965 it was possible to buy a five-story house, twenty feet wide, in fairly good shape and with decent architectural character, on an attractive street, at the following prices: $15,000, $27,000, $60,000, and $125,000. It was only a matter of whether it was located in the Lower East Side, Chelsea, Greenwich Village, or the Upper East Side. For the most part, fashions were dictating prices. These fashions have currently led property east of Central Park to become much more valuable than similar property west of the park. The odd thing is that at the time they were built, the row houses west of Central Park were mostly the finer, single-family buildings, while those east were largely unpretentious houses planned for several families.

When fashions in real estate are as marked as they are in New York, dense rebuilding takes place rapidly in order to get as much income as possible from a good address. In the case of Sutton Place, Lower Fifth Avenue, Washington Square, Gramercy Park and a large part of Greenwich Village, opportunistic redevelopment to exploit fashions has all but obliterated whatever substantial virtues were once present in these neighborhoods. Often the very buildings which helped set the initial character are replaced.

9

Private transfer of property is almost always governed by limited objectives, which may be contrary to general objectives such as the public welfare. At present in New York almost the entire urban environment can be disposed of as private owners wish. In contrast, medieval guilds protected towns against unreasonable and unnecessary change, often by controlling title to the land. The existence and disposition of every building was a matter of public concern, and sound use was therefore imperative.

Expendability and property

It also happens that modern technology and advanced architectural understanding can provide highly refined and particularized buildings, if not yet freely expendable ones. The availability of this talent for specialization acts as a catalyst toward change, especially since there is often a real need for specialized accommodation. Building users no longer have to be satisfied with general-purpose spaces when architects can give them new buildings that are individual as well as flexible.

Specialization

The modern implications of these questions of expendability and property seem clear. With changing user needs, land of high value, free powers of change in private hands, and ready accessibility of the means, the demand for the ever-increasing expendability of architecture is inevitable. And the onslaught for change must first affect the most venerable buildings in town.

More inevitable economic forces come into play because of the expanding requirements of society in management operations. The corporations, institutions and government offices located in New York are constantly seeking more space as their responsibilities grow. They need to provide for more people, with more complex jobs, communicating more efficiently. And meeting this problem is in fact the crux of a city's operation. These organizations must expand or perish, and since the contribution they make to the urban situation is vital, no city administrator would prevent them from expanding, or force them to move elsewhere to do so.

Requirements of management

Unfortunately, management organizations are made to compete for living space not only with each other, but with different vital facilities of the city — an unequal battle. The unrefined use restrictions of New York's fire codes and zoning laws seem effective in barring law offices and painters' studios from areas designated as residential, but they haven't withstood the pressures that forced Park Avenue between 45th Street and 59th Street into commercial occupancy. In that complex change, fashion made a residential area become commercially desirable. Once the encroachment of offices had begun, no attempt was made to conserve any of the centrally located housing, or even to encourage housing and offices to exist side by side as in European cities. The city cooperated by permitting zoning to change from residential to business use. The very high land values, created by fashion, rebuilt the whole section as offices in a few years.

Changing social and urban values also make for inevitable forces that alter the city. Reasonable demands of the city's inhabitants for greater amenity are now constantly being heard, ever more reasonably. If it is finally deemed proper for the city to have small park-squares every few blocks, some big questions of demolition will have to be weighed in the balance. The land adjacent to park-squares would thereby greatly increase in value — perhaps enough to pay for the tax and property loss.

Changing cultural values

Fresh social and urban values may lead to more community centers, more places of public assembly and leisure. Except for borough halls and county courthouses and the like, the outlying city districts lack almost everything worthy of civic pride or community attachment. Now almost *everything* must be sought in midtown Manhattan.

Museums and libraries must still largely depend on private charities to support them, and have not expanded because of the limits of their resources. The city universities have not grown much. These are

10

all latent but potentially active forces for change in New York, still waiting for new cultural values to find them.

Planned change Planning is necessary if a city is not to remain static, locked forever in the 18th or 19th century, unresponsive to the modern and future needs of its population. A full discussion of modern planning theory would be out of place here — there have been whole books about the Federal Urban Renewal program alone — but the subject deserves brief comment, because vast changes in cities are occurring increasingly as a result of full-scale planning, though not vast in New York so far.

Many planning theorists have written on the form and nature of the city, in attempts to explain its workings and improve its qualities. It often happens that discussions about improving the functional workings of the city lead immediately to proposals for an ideal new city form. Such discussions are more suited to new cities than existing ones. Undoubtedly a few revolutionary planning theories have been brilliant and influential — Ebenezer Howard's, for example. But frequently the result has been that some *revolutionary* schemes have been swallowed in part by *existing* cities, whatever the intentions of their authors.

The most famous revolutionary theorist, and one whose intentions were perfectly clear, was Le Corbusier. The full model for his ideal city was to be built over Paris. Hating the chaos and dirt and disorder, he designed a Radiant City to take its place. Huge buildings would be set vast distances apart in great parks. The streets of the city would have infrequent intersections to permit cars to move at rapid speeds between buildings. The "front door" of each giant house would admit hundreds or thousands.

Le Corbusier wrote a book about New York, *When the Cathedrals Were White.** When the cathedrals were white, he said, men had built with fresh vision. New York inspired him to think of his Radiant City again. The height, the gridiron of streets, the promise of change excited him. "New York is not a finished or completed city," he wrote. "It gushes up. On my next trip it will be different." The vision followed him home, and back, again and again, in 1920, and 1926, and 1928, and 1939. "I cannot forget New York, a vertical city, now that I have had the happiness of seeing it there, raised up in the sky." Unlike Paris, there was no lack of industry, and no reluctance to experiment. "New York has such courage and enthusiasm that everything can be begun again, sent back to the building yard and made into something greater, something mastered! These people are not on the point of going to sleep. In reality, the city is hardly more than twenty years old, that is the city which I am talking about, the city which is vertical and on the scale of the new times." When he looked for a moment among the towers, he was impatient with what he saw: "Between the present skyscrapers there are masses of large and small buildings. Most of them are small. What are these small houses doing in dramatic Manhattan? I haven't the slightest idea. It is incomprehensible. It is a fact, nothing more, as the debris after the earthquake or bombardment is a fact." There was no need to be held back by this. "A considerable part of New York is nothing more than a provisional city. A city which will be replaced by another city."

Yet from time to time, somewhere amid the enthusiasm and impatience and revolutionary fervor, there appears the other Le Corbusier, the humane witness. For page after page he goes on about sweeping away the past, then suddenly is distracted by something that suggests continuous existence. He takes the measure of the people that he sees and declares them ready, if any ever was, to sweep away the dead past; but in the next breath he praises the architectural spectacle and historic sensibility of the bronze statue of

---

* Reynal and Hitchcock, 1947.

Washington on the Sub-Treasury steps, in front of a Doric porch, in the canyon of Wall Street. One Le Corbusier hates the half-heartedness of it all, the only *provisional* Radiant City. The other Le Corbusier is enchanted by the accident and diversity of building. "A hundred times I have thought: New York is a catastrophe, and fifty times: it is a beautiful catastrophe."

When the Cathedrals Were White is a most compelling example of a revolutionary proposal for city change. No consideration detains the author's impatience to sweep away and begin again. The splendor of the necessary acts of destruction are almost magnificent in themselves — small wonder that some planners find ruthless change fascinating. Yet I believe that every idea is false except the perhaps essential one: that the principle of adaptation exists in the place itself; that, as he said, "the new times will discover the law of tomorrow in the furnace of cities." What Le Corbusier sought and found in New York was a fundamental principle — one of the New York things. His discovery was that New York is the city that should have been and perhaps yet will be the white city in the sky foretold by its history. But the crux of the matter is whether his proposal is the apotheosis and justification of that history, or the destroyer of it.

III.   All city change in New York is monitored, if not exactly regulated. Government powers exist not only in overt planning, but covertly influence every property decision. New York has powers of taxation, building codes, fire and health regulations, zoning laws, rent control laws, planning procedures, and preservation policies (now supported by law). Most of these are established in terms of restrictions rather than requirements, but in practice they move building and real estate in certain directions. For example, since buildings are currently being appraised for taxation on the basis of how prestigious they are, rather than on the basis of their actual value (as revealed in an appraisal of the Seagram Building*), it is obviously public policy to reward undistinguished building, a lesson not lost to speculative builders.

Building codes and fire and health regulations are primarily established to protect life and promote safety. By setting up inflexible standards they can also eliminate certain economical possiblities and force other action. Some stirring examples of how these codes may influence a city's form can be seen in New York. The water towers on almost every roof and the fire escapes, which are virtually a New York trademark, are creatures of these codes.

Building, fire, and health regulations

Zoning regulations are designed to advance the general welfare of the community through an overall system of land controls that protects the usefulness and value of property, and that tries to promote orderly community growth. New York's original Zoning Law of 1916, one of the earliest in the country, was

Zoning

---

* A few years after it was built the owners of the Seagram Building, Park Avenue between 52nd and 53rd Street, discovered that New York City was assessing their property for taxation as though the entire street floor land was covered with building and earning rent. Seagram took the matter to court, claiming the open space was a plaza and a civic contribution. The court upheld the city. It found that Seagram either planned the open space for prestige, or was demonstrating poor business acumen; and in either case the city was entitled to taxes based on the hypothetical full development.

replaced by a completely new law in 1960. The earlier experience had indicated how valuable a tool good zoning policy might be. The new law was an attempt to bring controls up to date.

Both old and new Zoning Laws deal with building use, bulk and area. The *use* to which a parcel of land may be put is obviously a matter of public concern, if a slaughterhouse or a chemical factory is not to appear next to an apartment house. The *bulk* is important if good light and fresh air are to be maintained for the adjacent property and streets. The *area* of the land covered by building is important for similar reasons. When zoning law was based primarily on requirements of health and general welfare and elimination of nuisance, these principles could not be faulted. But the new law, encouraged by recent court decisions permitting zoning for aesthetic purposes, has tried to legislate for civic beauty as well.

Since the old *bulk* requirements were bringing about "ziggurats" and "wedding cakes," complicated tiered buildings that just fit the "envelopes" of prescribed daylight angles, the new law established calculations for determining allowable bulk that encouraged the building of sheer slabs, presumably more tasteful shapes. (This was in post-Lever House days. It might never have happened if the artful setbacks of the Daily News or RCA buildings were still fresh in the mind.) To make sure that speculative builders played the game, the new law encouraged them to set back their towers from the street, and for compensation could add to the bulk by other complicated formulae. In the new law, the street setback is known as a "plaza." These setbacks are the reason why the present section of Sixth Avenue in the Fifties looks so uncharacteristic of New York. The new towers there — in imitation of Seagram, but unlike it — stand in very uncertain relation to the avenue, violating the strong lines of the streets with their "plazas." They create no real spaces as they upstage each other. They and the buildings overhead contribute nothing to the linear nature of the avenue, the "endless architecture" that is one of New York's greatest visual strengths. Sometimes buildings should be walls, not towers. The new Zoning Law encourages otherwise.

In the new area requirements for buildings, large scale projects are heavily favored. In order to get any allowable area to build upon that makes economic sense, several of the old New York land parcels must usually be assembled into one site. This means, for example, that a typical brownstone row house is now obsolete in New York's zoning. It couldn't be built in midtown under the new law, because it would cover too much land — too great a percentage, and would be hemmed in by other regulations invented to fit larger properties. But very much taller residential buildings could be built, provided several old brownstones parcels are assembled. Far more dwelling units than there were in the old brownstones can be built on the combined lot under the new law. The scale of building — and the relationship of building to street — would have to change. Needless to say, such a proposition promotes the acquisition of many small properties such as brownstones, with great profit incentive for their clearance and replacement.

Rent control The most insidious force for destruction in New York has been the Rent Control Law. Whatever the merits and justifications for setting standard rents, the fact that a free rental market is permitted to exist alongside the controlled market has caused New York to lose, and will make it continue to lose, some of its most distinguished and essential architecture.

The present Rent Control Law is now administered by the city, but it is a descendant of national wartime price controls. According to the law, housing and commercial rentals in most buildings over a certain age are fixed, subject to board review. The rentals can be increased up to 15% upon change of tenancy, or because of increased services, or if the landlord is not getting at least a 6% return on his investment. They can be decreased if services are decreased. In a situation where there is not enough housing to go around, such a law is worthwhile, since it protects tenants from inflated rents and safeguards their occu-

13

pancy. Even under the present circumstances, when city housing has become less scarce, the law still preserves the stability of communities, and a social balance among people of different incomes is maintained by widely different rents within the market.

The law has often been criticized; not only by real estate groups, but also by disinterested observers. Some feel that the law should be changed because communities have become *too* stable; for example (a much-heard example), older couples will usually hold large apartments after their children have left home, simply because their continuous tenancy maintains their low rent. Others believe that the law should be abolished or gradually eliminated, since an unregulated housing market is somehow "better" than a regulated one. The wishes of these last critics have been fulfilled, causing the unmitigated disaster that has befallen some of the city's best buildings.

Besides the buildings under Rent Control, there were always some not controlled at all. At first they were only those accommodations — never in short supply in New York — which were very expensive. A free market existed in that rarified air. But upon pressure for gradual disengagement from controls, all *new* building was kept out of Rent Control. It was thought that since the new buildings would have to compete in rents with controlled ones, their rents would stay down during the period of transition. But what in fact has been happening, with impeccable economic logic, is a sort of Gresham's Law of building — bad buildings are driving out good. Any new cheap construction can command higher permitted rents than better buildings formerly in the same place. Thus commodious town houses are being demolished to make way for economy apartment buildings, because a floor in the former produces less rent than a flat in the latter.

Since the early 1950s, whole sections of New York have been transformed by such new building. Developers have been buying up rent-controlled properties as fast as they can, all over the East Side and the Village and wherever they think the neighborhood might support far higher rents. They tear them down, and in their place cheaply constructed "luxury" apartment houses soon appear. To keep the costs of total rents within rational limits, apartment sizes are minimal. A socially disproportionate number of "efficiency" apartments and one-bedroom ("4-room") apartments are crammed into a typical building.

This is not the building program that the city needs. If the Rent Control Law continues to exist in the future, it ought to include all buildings and it should serve merely as a set of limits which prohibits a drastic rise in city rents. Since the Rent Control Law has excluded new construction, the only question now is how long it will take before all the old New York buildings are down. As long as the law provides that they are in the way of profit, it is just a matter of time.

While the City Planning Commission and the Department of City Planning are nominally responsible for promoting good order in the city, many other agencies have exercised some of the same powers. Among them are the Department of Marine and Aviation, the Traffic Department, and the various borough presidents' offices, inside the municipal government; outside it there are the Triborough Bridge and Tunnel Authority, the Port of New York Authority and the Tri-State Transportation Commission. All of these except the last (which is at present restricted to planning exclusively) are engaged in practical operations as well as theoretical proposals. Since even such city departments as the Board of Education, the Department of Parks, and the Department of Water Supply may plan and build on their own, it is easy to see how disordered the New York planning process can get to be. In the past, crucial decisions were often made to suit whichever agency had the most influence with the mayor. Other times, several agencies would be in conflict, and each would act autonomously. And then some of the most far-reaching decisions, affecting basic city form or calling for substantive settlement of questions of public policy, have

Planning authorities

14

been put over by the independent Authorities or have been agreed upon by the city administration without consulting the electorate. It is obvious even to its present practitioners that planning by conflict and competition among parties which have their own vital interests to promote, done with as much secrecy from the public as possible, is the very worst way to plan. The fact that it has led to irrational change and needless destruction of the city's form is also obvious.

The preservation
law

Since 1965 New York has had a Landmarks Preservation Law. The law provides that a Landmarks Preservation Commission may from time to time designate city Landmarks, and that no Landmark thus designated can be demolished or altered on the exterior without the consent of the Commission. Some procedures are mentioned in the law for financial aid in cases where maintenance of a Landmark interferes with an owner's profit. Purchase by the city is suggested if no other assistance is enough. With this law, New York joined over seventy other American cities which had already enacted municipal preservation legislation.

At the time the law was passed, about 750 individual Landmarks were being considered for protection, based on a Commission survey of the five boroughs of Greater New York. A few score have since been designated. The Landmarks are mostly "monuments" rather than buildings of unpretentious character, but some whole districts are additionally listed, such as sections of Brooklyn Heights, Greenwich Village, and the cast-iron commercial area.

At this moment it is hard to say what effect the law will have on checking wanton destruction. It is a good law, strong because its policy is based on governing powers rather than compensation. The theory is that a Landmark is part of the public patrimony, and an owner need not be bribed to preserve it. However, the problems of economic distress are recognized and compensation for such is suggested.

There are two major flaws in the preservation law. One is that it deals entirely with external appearance. Many buildings are far more significant in their interiors — Grand Central Station and the 39th Street Metropolitan Opera, for example. Preservation for such as these ought to be based on maintaining the interiors as well. The other flaw is in the nature of a last-minute insertion in the bill under enactment, a "moratorium clause." It provides that Landmarks can be designated only at three-year intervals, a gaping escape hatch for shrewd wreckers.

Early reaction to the law has been severe. Many institutions, such as the New York Stock Exchange and some church groups, find themselves embarrassed to be owning Landmarks, with some of their property rights now under regulation. Several of the first Landmark designations certainly suggest that the Commission is unafraid of protest. But by failing to designate the old Metropolitan Opera House (see page 206), they have indicated their unwillingness to be swayed by the most familiar of objections: those made by owners who arrange to sell in order to rebuild. Having made a lucrative deal for the old property, the Metropolitan Opera Association was determined to have no interference from anyone. They didn't want the building anymore, nor did they wish any other opera company to inherit it, so for their part, it had to be torn down to provide a site for an office building, and a sum of money for the not bereaved opera trustees.

Application
of powers

The fact that many government powers have been used in the destruction of much of New York's essential form doesn't mean that these powers should be abolished or curtailed if preservation is to be more successful. But proper application of powers is everything. If they are contradictory, arbitrary or misapplied, the blind force of legislation and police power are more destructive than *laissez-faire*. They are forces that suicidally increase the self-destructive nature of a modern city, beyond the random injurious acts of the accident-prone.

If considerations of continuity and a sense of the past are to have influence, then there must be someone with the responsibility of determining what things are essential to the city. Measures should be taken to conserve those things from the vicissitudes of heedless change. In New York, concern about the form of the city is obviously part of the jobs of many people, and yet none has particular responsibility. The City Planning Commission is not responsible for *carrying out* plans, and in any case even their wishes may not be followed by the mayor. While the Triborough and Port Authorities do build what they plan, they have bondholders to serve, whose interests do not necessarily coincide with those of the public. The Landmarks Preservation Commission is by law empowered to preserve. But a few score monuments are not a city. If these are all they can hold on to, it is obviously no safeguard against heedless change.

The main responsibility should, however, be that of planners. A planner must be concerned not only with what changes, but with what must not change. Consideration of the second is often forgotten. It is the harder part of a planner's responsibility. The practice of planning, in drafting offices far from the situation, makes it easy to forget about what is to remain. It is easier to create form than to adapt it, easier to ignore possibilities than to struggle with them. It is actually even easier to change than not to change. But when circumstances seem to compel change, this is the moment when the designer has to carefully reflect. Is the corrective necessary?

If a dozen separate agencies control building in New York, and among them can't guarantee the preservation of New York's essential form, then it may be time to attack policy-making by specialists. For want of clear *general* thinking, some urgent and fundamental considerations have obviously never been directed to any of the specialists' offices. But this failure of initiative may be partly a good thing. It is timely, before New York planning overhauls itself and becomes cooperative and efficient, to remember that many of the things planners have been called upon to decide are not matters for experts at all. Preservation and the limits of change are general matters of broad import, which the public at large has every right to discuss. (The explanation often heard for concealment of plans from the public is that full exposure may drive up property prices — a shockingly meager excuse, considering government powers of eminent domain.) An Authority should not have the autonomous authority to decide that eviction of people from their homes is necessary to facilitate some work — as happens now. A great deal could be said about the new "displacement" approach of much public planning, and the sort of disordered lives, neighborhoods, and social systems it is likely to produce. But such problems would not come up so frequently if the people concerned, according to every definition of democracy, were being consulted.

Once the general goals of the city and proposals for comprehensive adaptation are openly debated in the community, the city planner's technical job could begin. Being responsible for continuity, he would have to make the detailed decisions about conservation and change, within the guidelines established by the public policy. Since he would be under a more directly democratic procedure he would be unable to resort to sweeping clearance and upheaval techniques, and his work would become much more complicated and difficult than it already is. Many stages of development would need to be set, and the parts planned for the remoter future might have multiple alternatives. The very complexity of his task would suggest some immediate conservation policies.

This could be done on the basis set down by Sir Patrick Geddes in his 1915–19 reports on Indian towns.*

---

* *Patrick Geddes in India*, edited by Jacqueline Tyrwhitt (London: Percy Lund, Humphries & Co., Ltd., 1947).

Geddes believed that to disregard tradition was a vulgarity. He called for "conservative surgery" as an economical approach toward change, condemning the policy of sweeping clearances.

The English architect-planners Peter and Alison Smithson were faced squarely with the same question — conserving the essential city — in a 1962 study they made of Cambridge. Cambridge University was not only the center, but the basis for the town's growth and continued existence. Yet the lives and work of many people were unconnected with the University. In putting down some general thoughts arising from a consideration of Cambridge, Alison Smithson contemplated the multiple paths of people's lives, the sometimes striking limitations of planning in being able to select, order and define, and the incredibly strong patterns of life structured by forms of the past. Here she writes not primarily of Cambridge, but of all cities:

> Conservation could have a real freeing power in our cities. By conserving intact for periods of ten, twenty or forty years such areas that still offer viable human environment — even if its exact nature is indefinable in administrative terms (no more definable than 'the right smell') — there could be established 'fixes' which would cut the field of action for creative planning down to manageable size. The conserved area-fixes would be continual reminders of the right scale of thinking, elucidating at all stages the elusiveness of 'good environment.' Area-fixes would tend to channel creative planning into areas whose environment has been totally invalidated.
> In between such areas of conservation and areas of strict guidance forming new environment might then come defined areas neither worth conserving nor clear yet in which way they could usefully be replanned. These might be free of certain planning control for periods of twenty, forty or eighty years, to become experimental areas in which the forces at work could play an ultimate programming role.
> Such aids to comprehension of the actual task also allow concentration of available intellect, capital and energy into special areas . . . An open system, one not aimed at a levelling off environment, could make better use of the truly different talents people possess.*

Preservationism

A name that can be given to one kind of limited protection of a city's essential form is *preservationism*. Within its meaning, monuments are considered for their historical value or their architectural importance, but essentially for their own sake. The building becomes the issue of importance rather than its uses. It must be defended as an *object*. The New York preservation law takes notice of Landmark sites, but they are defined and defended in relation to the Landmark itself. It also seeks to protect "Historic Districts." Even though these are environmental rather than individual, appearance and not use is what matters. They are designated as Historic Districts because they have special character or special historical or aesthetic interest, *and* because they represent one or more periods or styles of architecture. In other words, whole Historic Districts are also determined solely by the importance of the buildings as objects. By selecting them as objects, only the external aspects — literally and figuratively — are being defended. Their appearance is preserved by protecting "exterior architectural features."

---

* *Team 10 Primer*, edited by Alison Smithson (London: Standard Catalogue Co., 1965).

Economic survival is sometimes very difficult for Landmarks. The uses of the Landmark and the entire district may change, or may have already changed. Whatever the economic chances for maintaining a historic building when the use remains the same, those chances are usually much reduced when the original use has disappeared and the environment has radically altered. New York's "Old Merchant's House" on East 4th Street is difficult to preserve, if only as a museum, because the old, elegant residences of nearby Lafayette Place (now Street — see page 130) have been supplanted by commercial lofts. The district even lacks the vitality of that kind of use, for not many appreciative visitors come by.

Whatever the reasons for cherishing them, many of the most valuable elements of a city are those buildings which are wonderful for their own sakes. They may be so bound up with the city's history, or so representative of the spirit of a certain time, or so beautiful as buildings alone, that their loss is unthinkable. Such buildings certainly deserve to be defended as objects in their own right. They should be sorted out from the rest, protected and preserved for their singularity. They may be monuments more than "Landmarks," since their present situation is often irrelevant, but it is a worthy and urgent part of any city's responsibility to preserve them. Preservationism must be a component of protecting a city's essential form.

An equally fundamental aspect of protection can be distinguished as *conservationism*. If this principle is firmly established and operating smoothly, there is no need for emergency rescue, indignant editorials, or financial support. It can be accomplished by nurturing rather than trying to reimpose urban continuity.

Conservationism

If cast-iron Worth Street (see page 164) had continued to be the partial home of the textile industry, for example — if the industry had been encouraged to remain in that area, with zoning favoring the trade and fire regulations coaxing improvement of the property rather than abandonment of it — then perhaps that would have been enough to keep the industry from moving uptown. Demand for new commercial space might have been directed against ramshackle real estate in the vicinity, and Worth Street, the historic center, could have been designated for preservation if necessary. The chances are that legal preservation would then have been only a safeguard, and not a necessity.

Worth Street was architecturally meritorious when the buildings were used merely as lofts. Rehabilitated as corporate offices, the street would have been one of the greatest ensembles in America — and would have presented an aspect that the invisible images of "Madison Avenue," "Wall Street," and, sadly, "Seventh Avenue" lack entirely. When most of Worth Street was demolished for a parking lot a few years ago, timely preservation legislation could have saved it. But the infinitely more complex and finally more gratifying measures of urban conservation should have been used to begin with.

The ideal way of establishing a sense of continuity in cities combines both preservation and conservation — different but compatible techniques. One of the tasks of municipal government should be to promote thrift through the conservation of urban form. This can be done with the intelligent exercise of existing government powers.

And why not urban conservation? We recognize the need to conserve every other aspect and resource of our environment. Ultimately, a stand of Douglas Fir or Redwood is more easily replaceable than the forms that evoke a bit of human history. Conservation is not necessarily an act practiced by conservatives. It is concerned with the search for best use as well as thrift. It calls for active perception and timely and imaginative decisions if anything is to pay off. If the best use is to be made of urban resources, there has to be endless vigilance by city planners. It is, in a way, the opposite of preservationism, where a law is passed in a moment and then the constant job of holding back change begins. In urban conservation, the work to use things to best advantage is continuous. Only the rewards are simple and self-accomplished.

Survival for the essential city

What needs to be sought and conserved are the basic things in the city, the truthful things measured by human experience, though not necessarily those most clear and well-ordered and visual. These should be things that state the case of the city from its birth — things which, in summary, have been called here the city's "essential form." The solution to the problem of survival should begin with an analysis of what that essential form is, and the public must participate in the discussion.

A conservation program can then be performed by elected officials and planners. They need to be as circumspect in the prevention of waste as careful naturalists or ecologists, and as considerate of life. They need to be preoccupied with the entire system, history and structure of the city — and seek not only to improve its operations and extend its possibilities, but to conserve its natural and unnatural resources. They not only must be able to change the form of the city, they must also defend it — by practicing *conservation of form*. The second is the more difficult job.

Towards the essential New York

In New York, Le Corbusier believed, change was the fixed condition. Its basic nature, character, steady state was change; what got saved and preserved was a radical variable. New York to him was "A city which will be replaced by another city." It is very likely indeed that change is one of the fundamental New York characteristics. It was one of the great, disturbing symbols of Herzog's world in Saul Bellow's novel. Moses Herzog is forever passing scenes of demolition. Park Avenue is filled with construction machinery and smells of cement. The city is summed up by a series of taxi rides and walks through dust:

At the corner he paused to watch the work of the wrecking crew. The great metal ball swung at the walls, passed easily through brick, and entered the rooms, the lazy weight browsing on kitchens and parlors. Everything it touched wavered and burst, spilled down. There rose a white tranquil cloud of plaster dust. The afternoon was ending, and in the widening area of demolition was a fire, fed by the wreckage. Moses heard the air, softly pulled toward the flames, felt the heat. The workmen, heaping the bonfire with wood, threw strips of moulding like javelins. Paint and varnish smoked like incense. The old flooring burned gratefully — the funeral of exhausted objects. Scaffolds walled with pink, white, green doors quivered as the six-wheeled trucks carried off fallen brick. The sun, now leaving for New Jersey and the west, was surrounded by a dazzling broth of atmospheric gases. Herzog observed that people were spattered with red stains, and that he himself was flecked on the arms and chest. He crossed Seventh Avenue and entered the subway.*

If perpetual change is the destiny of New York, it might not have to be at the cost of such devastation and bloodletting. Believing it to be the price of progress, New Yorkers are remarkably cheerful about destruction. They have faith that their city is in the process of adapting itself better to their needs, even if the reverse may be true.

Perpetual change is just as difficult to live with as perpetual unchange. The city of Venice faces the other problem. The entire city is treated as a museum, and since there is no intention of materially altering it, the lives of its citizens must be adapted to whatever can be made of the old city form — mostly tourism

---

* Saul Bellow, *Herzog*, Viking Press, 1964.

and old crafts, with essential services. They are committed everlastingly to the same urban order of things that served well centuries before. The frozen past is undoubtedly a curse and hardship for many. Yet should the world be deprived of Venice? Should Italy? Should those of its inhabitants who love it? Perhaps the question of change in both New York and Venice is resolved by the fact that a city ultimately selects its own people. Those who live in Venice do so partly because it is unlike anyplace else.

Most New Yorkers who have been chosen by their city are prepared to accept economic imperatives as sufficient reason for change. Fortunately, the economics of building are the easiest to manipulate in order to favor beneficial change. Government is already doing it with taxes and laws and regulations. But it is still considered a rather radical idea to expect these uncoordinated powers to help carry out planning policy instead of, as frequently happens, obstructing it.*

Future change

In New York's early planning, the form of the city was established as a linear development, moving north from the tip of Manhattan Island. That this was indeed fundamental and prophetic was demonstrated by the fact that through *laissez-faire* action alone, the center of gravity of the city moved uptown to 23rd Street, 34th Street, 59th Street. There it stopped, and later growth has been mostly accompanied by self-destruction. But here lies a useful principle. If postwar planning had been concerned with urban conservation, it might have been possible to direct the explosive expansion of management facilities up to Central Park North or perhaps Fordham Road in the Bronx, instead of letting it destroy part of Park Avenue. Indeed, the expansion might have moved any place in the city, north or south, which was weak in form but well situated and well connected with transportation.

Public transit, present or contemplated, might be providing the matrix for change. Year by year, a complex of new facilities for the movement of people and goods should be carried forward as part of a development plan. When new intersections on the transit matrix have been established, both public improvement and heavy incentives to private investment should follow. New York has miles and miles of nebulous suburbs to spare. The time and effort of building should be directed towards making them identifiable city subcenters, instead of eradicating the existing city.

New York, as well as other cities, can fulfill its destiny through changing its weakest elements. These are the things that are unessential in terms of the present or the past. The evolving form of the city ought to be an affirmation of the relevance of life to the uniqueness of the place.

Postscript 2000

Technology has recently provided us with revolutionary opportunities for change. Anything can be built, moved, or destroyed. Now is the last possible moment for resisting the acts of destruction that would separate us finally from earlier experience. For unlike history, unlike politics or philosophy or even art, the environment allows the actual experience of cultural continuity to be felt — an experience to be cherished by children as much as (or perhaps more than) by savants and scholars.

---

* As an example, there is no reason for real estate taxes to be uniform. They might be zoned by a planning body to correspond with development needs, perhaps with a ten-year lag to permit adjustment, and as a precaution against improper use of the power.

Ultimately, the need for change, like anything else in building, ought to be determined by the needs of the users. Where the city form is concerned, not only are the owners of a particular property the users but also everyone who passes and sees it. Existing places are truly *time-honored*. Strictly speaking, everything is time-honored and ought to be considered as such when change is contemplated. But of all things, certainly architecture has aspects most concerned with time. Architecture provides the only measurable way to discover the past in the urban environment, and its conservation is therefore not only expedient but vital. A city can be complete and unique only in relation to its own history and essential form, and this must be reawakened, discovered anew, or sought and defended. That is the form of creative destruction that would be creative, not just destructive.

To put it in the largest terms, our lives minute by minute are a confusion of events and feelings. Only in reference to the past do we discern the story's plot. Where in the world do we obtain this information? From the stimuli of memorable places and experiences. In the countryside there is a nearly endless present, with the cycle of seasons as the bare plot. In a city, where the natural world is mainly concealed, a rich plot derives from its development compared to ours, its persistence with ours.

Without plots, we move like termites through the dark cellulose of time, chewing but hardly understanding. Through memory, we are able to develop vision and judgment and begin to catch on. Plots aren't like quotidian life. They're fiction. But because they derive from the past, they give us the greatest sense of a foreseeable future with our place assured.

THE URBAN SCENE AND PUBLIC PLACES.

The Greek agora, the medieval marketplace, and the Italian piazza served their cities by providing convenient places where human interaction naturally occurred. These squares originated in the need for public assembly, and were situated in the principal centers of activity. New York's natural meeting places are far less formal. With the city's regular blocks and relatively wide sidewalks, paths and purposes can interact along the street (on front steps, around pushcarts, on avenues during a lunch hour); in the neighborhood parks and playgrounds (particularly at the promenades lined with benches that are adjacent to buildings); or at railroad stations, airports, even at taxi stands outside hotels. These are all public places in the sense that they provide for interaction and encounter. It is characteristic of New York that an informal public nexus is usually a point along a route, a place to pause before moving on to the next destination.

Like most American cities, New York would benefit from having more places planned for casual public encounter. But once it becomes clear that public places need not be narrowly defined as primarily architectural or monumental in character, measures can be taken to conserve the vitality of those we now have. Vitality can be eroded. A conservation program should guard against even the seemingly trivial changes in urban operations that reduce the richness of use. For example, making city avenues one-way discourages the casual stroller because of the intrusion of faster and noisier vehicular traffic. The same act moves bus routes to alternate avenues, often 1600 feet apart, thus halving the opportunity of access to buses. Yet multiple opportunities are exactly what city streets need to remain vital.

Some parts of New York's urban scene are famous throughout the world. The skyline and downtown canyons of the financial district are magnificent because they are vivid, practical and unique. They are a clear representation of commercial enterprise, valuable land, and the necessity of good communications. It is significant that they grew up in a direct self-determined way, before limitations were set on the bulk and height of buildings. As a testament to the essential formation of New York, this part of the urban scene provides us with some straightforward truth about the city.

"Space in the image of man is *place*," says the architect Aldo van Eyck. Public places are created by human use, not the other way around. Clear urban configurations reveal significant characteristics of human use adapted to the place. Usually those characteristics which most clearly depict essential aspects of the city are those best loved. They throb with life created by history, but seem quite free of time.

The Grand Army Plaza, or as it is usually called, the Plaza — the widening of Fifth Avenue before Central Park. The Plaza Hotel (right), an earlier namesake of the present building on the same spot, was begun in 1881 by the firm of Fife and Campbell, but was held up for eight years by litigation. It opened in 1890, but then closed in 1905, to be demolished and replaced by architect Henry J. Hardenbergh's Plaza two years later. The Plaza fountain, designed by Thomas Hastings and topped with Karl Bitter's statue of "Abundance," was not built until 1916 upon Joseph Pulitzer's $50,000 bequest.

1

2

THE PLAZA'S PLAZA.   Most of the great European squares are spaces defined by their walls; that is to say, it is enclosure that matters. The character of the square is distinguished mainly by the architecture surrounding it, and buildings give the open space its scale and form. However, in New York's Plaza almost all the buildings which form the surrounding walls have been replaced one or more times. The Hotel Netherland (1, right), north of 59th Street, was supplanted by the Sherry-Netherland. Leading to the square, "Marble Row," an elegant street of individual town houses (see pages 26 and 124) which ran between 57th and 58th Streets on the east side of Fifth Avenue (2, left), is now gone. Most splendid of all the Plaza's vanished buildings was Cornelius Vanderbilt's mansion, directly to the south (3, and see pages 111 and 121).

Some of the earlier buildings which are "lost" here were fortunately not elements fundamental to the Plaza as an urban space. The secret of the Plaza, and its character and importance, really lies not in buildings but in the New York grid of streets which is so seldom interrupted by anything, especially by a green space. Here at last Fifth Avenue breaks loose from two walls and, at 58th Street, opens wide into a three-sided square before it gets to the vaster freedom of Central Park a block to the north. The generator of this singular urban space is the traffic system. Only the Plaza Hotel, by accident the longest-lasting element on the scene, functions in architectural terms. Though the hotel was named for the square, the square now seems a forecourt for the hotel, and the building becomes a pivot-point at two crucial streets.

What should have remained essential, given the Plaza's geometrical basis of streets and buildings, was the force of the street lines. However, on the site of the 1927 McKim, Mead and White Savoy-Plaza Hotel (4, left), the General Motors building came along in the 1960s, with an egregious piazzetta setting back the footprint of the new tower.

3   4

TRIUMPHAL ARCHES. The temporary wooden arch that Stanford White designed in 1889 for the centennial of George Washington's inauguration (1) proved a suitable terminus for Fifth Avenue at a time when the houses adjacent to Washington Square were low enough to stand modestly beside it (see page 42). White's later masonry arch is now permanently in place — not spanning the Avenue, but back into the Square. In 1892, the 400th anniversary of Columbus Day was celebrated with the temporary erection of a triumphal arch at Fifth Avenue and 57th Street (2 — Marble Row is at the right of the north-facing view). The plaster and wood arch built for the return of Admiral Dewey in 1899 (3) was a collaboration by G. R. Lamb, architect, with members of the National Sculpture Society. Fifth Avenue and 23rd Street was the site, and it was still important enough as a city nexus twenty years later to be chosen as the location for another parade structure, an Arch of Victory for the American Expeditionary Force.

Temporary festival structures are works which are generally associated with the late Renaissance and Baroque. Yet the idea of building a decorative arch, rather than a mere reviewing stand, still seems appropriate for public ceremonies — and the way the 23rd Street arches defined an amorphous street intersection indicated something that was even worth making permanent.

1 2   3

1   2

EARLY GRAND CENTRAL TERMINALS.   The first Grand Central (1) was built in 1871 for the New York and Harlem, New York and New Haven, and New York Central Railroads. The rugged mansard-roofed wings flanking a central block formed an outline imitated by the Grand Union Hotel, from which this photo was taken. The depot was enlarged in 1899, and redesigned by C. P. R. Gilbert according to the stylistic modes of its own decade (2). The acquisition of underground track rights in 1903 made the present terminal necessary.

1

THE GRAND CENTRAL SKYLINE.   The railroad tracks buried under Park Avenue established a new visual configuration for the avenue and for the buildings on it. The New York Central office building, its odd Gothic-style corbelled tower ending the vista, came to characterize Park Avenue (1), and appropriately so. With its outline and decoration, it was able to indicate clearly its relationship to the height of a man, and so was able to convey to the observer its own true size. It therefore was like an enormous measuring-rod, and from miles off along Park Avenue the dimensions of half a city could be

perceived with its help. This visual indicator, which explained scale so simply, was lost when the new Pan Am building obliterated the Park Avenue skyline with its own undifferentiated silhouette.

Scale and clarity are likewise fortified when important interior spaces are revealed as impressive volumes in the urban scene. The Grand Central Waiting Room and Concourse was a clear form which was coherently scaled when other buildings deferred to it (3), before the Pan Am building was built. Almost four blocks of distance could be judged between the sculptured entablature of the Terminal and the lanterned roof of the New York Central Building (4). And Warren & Wetmore's auto ramps, which carry Park Avenue on a breathtaking ride around Grand Central, were much more potent when there was more sky to be seen among the buildings (2).

PENNSYLVANIA STATION.   Work began on Penn Station in 1906, following the designs of McKim, Mead and White, with Charles Follen McKim as Partner-in-Charge. According to contemporary accounts, the "great quarry" made by the excavation was comparable to the building of the Panama Canal. The design was also a conscious enough attempt on the part of the Pennsylvania Railroad Company to establish the importance of railroads by building a pre-eminent building, a civic masterpiece. What the newspapers called an "undertaking without precedent" was therefore fairly considered to have exceeded the greatest public efforts of history.

When it was completed in 1910, New York had a station built with the grandeur of Rome (in fact, it was supposed to be a replica of the Caracalla Baths). But behind the ingenuous magniloquence of its facades (1) was the genuine majesty of its steel-ribbed spaces (7). The great Train Concourse was covered with acres of glass in domes, arches and vaults (2) — a free translation of masonry forms into the fragile elements of machine technology; and not so much in the academic tradition of historicism as in the new tradition of the Crystal Palaces and the glass galleries and halls of Paris exhibitions. This was the space the spectator saw as he arrived in New York: the corrugated glass roof arches and domes (3) and the main Concourse an open level above the tracks (4).

1

2

From there, before the addition of the tawdry new ticket office which closed the passage, the arriving visitor moved past the lesser waiting rooms into the General Waiting Room. He was confronted by an enormous vaulted space (5), this time done more conventionally with coffered plasterwork hung from the concealed steel structure. Telephones, parcel and ticket offices were located in this hall. A Lunch Room and more formal Dining Room (see page 56) lay beyond, flanking the grand staircase on the procession east — then along a lofty arcade to the vestibule and the street at Seventh Avenue. Alternatively, if the visitor had baggage and wanted a taxi, he could emerge directly from the General Waiting Room into a carriageway on either the north or south side of the station (6).

5

6

Mass Assembly and Mass Movement were clearly defined by the station, but it had also an undoubted nobility which it imparted to the observer — "Or did," commented Lewis Mumford, "until that structure was converted by its thoughtful guardians into a vast jukebox . . ." And yet it remained — a majestic threshold into the headquarters city for the traveler from Glen Cove or Chicago. It seemed as if it would take a new Flood to sweep it away.

"Until the first blow fell," the *New York Times* wrote on October 30, 1963, "no one was convinced that Penn Station really would be demolished or that New York would permit this monumental act of vandalism . . . Any city gets what it admires, will pay for, and ultimately deserves. Even when we had Penn Station, we couldn't afford to keep it clean. We want and deserve tin-can architecture in a tin-horn

7

8

9

culture. And we will probably be judged not by the monuments we build but by those we have destroyed."
The station was sacrificed through application of the real-estate logic that often dictates the demolition
of the very building that makes an area desirable (8, 9). In a letter to the *Times*, the President of the
Pennsylvania Railroad Company asked, "Does it make any sense to preserve a building merely as a
'monument'?"

1

CENTRAL PARK AS PLANNED.   In 1851, there was nothing that could be called a park in America. For a natural public place, New York had the parade ground at the Battery. The first suggestions for a large city park came from William Cullen Bryant, a town dweller who missed his rural pleasures, and from Andrew J. Downing, a landscape architect impressed with the parks of Europe. Mayor Kingsland became interested, and in 1853 the principle was approved by the New York Board of Aldermen. A competition was held in 1858, won by Frederick Law Olmsted and Calvert Vaux. By this time the site had been changed from a forested area along the East River to a rather barren tract in the center of the island, chiefly because it could be obtained at lower cost.

The sparseness of natural riches provided Olmsted and Vaux with the opportunity to design a park according to the precepts of English landscape gardening. One of the lessons taught by the British work of William Kent, Capability Brown, and Humphry Repton was that the creation of perfect natural landscape was essentially an artistic and artificial effort: a garden should be an earthly paradise, an Eden, a representation of nature in well-balanced perfection. Central Park's bare tract therefore was designed

2   3

to epitomize and condense the greatest possible variety of woods and water, tangles, cascades, and craggy heights. After the park had been built according to this plan and had been growing for forty years, a New York historian proudly directed attention to "the craft of the illusion and the perfection of the art that can produce such a panorama of Nature in so little space" (E. I. Zeisloft, *The New Metropolis*, 1899).

Olmsted's 800-acre landscape design depended on contrasts between wild and tamed parts, open vistas and densely planted sections. The dense planting (1, 3) began to be removed when New York police operations suggested the elimination of shrubbery that might conceal anybody. Appropriate park structures by Vaux and others — such as a bandstand (2) — have vanished, and the park has instead become a building site for dozens of anti-garden philanthropic monuments, from skating rinks and theaters to a grotesque "Children's Zoo."

One hears that the park is dangerous, and for a long time that became a self-fulfilling prophecy, as fewer and fewer went there, maintenance decreased, amenities vanished. Central Park, once a model of the perfection of nature, became an official maintenance problem — a natural one, like six inches of snow. For many years disposal was the treatment it received.

SCALE OF BUILDINGS TO STREETS. Fifth Avenue from the top of Washington Arch (1), until quite recently, was virtually the same quiet residential street that Henry James knew, even though familiar landmarks were vanishing. Soon after the period of his *Washington Square*, the Brevoort House was demolished (see page 117), and the Brevoort Hotel (the white building on the right-hand side of the street) began its slow decline before it met its dusty death. But when tall apartment houses were built on lower Fifth Avenue a few years ago, the new buildings finally shattered the relationship of building height to street width that was the street's essential characteristic. This has permanently

1

altered the walk-up scale and obviously residential character of a famous milieu.

A very different scale had been established on Park Avenue, where the great street width was made necessary by the underground New York Central tracks (2). Real park malls once ran down the center of Park Avenue's midtown area, bringing the width down to human size, and in scale with the existing residential buildings. The park malls were destroyed in 1927 when they were reduced to narrow traffic islands, in order to give motor vehicles more room. Almost all the buildings shown here have been replaced by office blocks, including the Sheraton East Hotel (right, beyond St. Bartholomew's Church).

2

PRIVATE
GATHERING PLACES.

Against William Penn's "The public must and will be served" can be set William H. Vanderbilt's "The public be damned!" as a remark perhaps more characteristic of New York. The public is actually served and damned in different ways, often for profit. Privately run accommodations are as socially essential as public places. They enclose important public activities such as political meetings, dining, playgoing, and in the past, even gambling. The only thing really "private" about a hotel or a meeting hall is its ownership.

Stanford White's Madison Square Garden, one of the most popular, useful, and worthwhile of buildings, provides a reasonable example. It was sold because the operators thought a cheaper building would be better able to pay its way, and since the site was in demand, cash was available. Under the circumstances complete financing was readily found for a new building, the old one was sold, and the new one went up. Based in part on the proceeds of the old building's sale, the new Garden was expected to show a satisfactory profit — a familiar story in real estate. But was it ever considered that the first building was better than the one that replaced it? Or that the original location adjacent to Madison Square Park was much more desirable, for the city's sake? If these matters had been responsibly taken into account, the outcome undoubtedly would have been different. Maintenance of worthwhile private gathering places is strongly in the public interest and should therefore be made attractive to owners by the city. But the basic responsibility for maintaining private property is a private one.

In changing aspects of cities there is a certain point where public interests can be completely neglected, and private operators allowed to dispose of their property as they wish. This point ought to be clearly defined as the place where all public access stops. Certainly the privilege of running a place of public accommodation for profit bears with it certain civic responsibilities. A private owner should be prepared to accept the legal necessity for practicing conservation on his own premises when the services he offers — including also the building that he has provided — turn out to be essential public commodities.

The 26th floor tower lounge of The Panhellenic, designed by John Mead Howells, was built in 1928 at First Avenue and 49th Street and subsequently called the Beekman Tower Hotel. The building has now been converted into apartments.

BROADWAY TABERNACLE. The Broadway Tabernacle stood at 340 to 344 Broadway, between Worth Street and Catherine Lane. It was built by a church society in 1836 to promote the growth of New England Congregationalism in New York, but its most memorable function was its service for a while as the city's main meeting hall. Many anti-slavery rallies were held at the Tabernacle, and numerous old prints show how frequently the hall was the scene of important public events. The view here is of the ratification meeting of Millard Fillmore as candidate of the American Party in 1856.

The Tabernacle was sold and demolished in 1857 to make way for a dry goods warehouse. Funds from the sale were used to build a neo-Gothic Congregational church at Sixth Avenue and 34th Street.

46

NIBLO'S GARDEN.   Nine blocks uptown from the Tabernacle was Niblo's Garden and Theater, at Broadway and Prince Street. It was built in 1827 and was first known as the Sans Souci. For a while the Garden was the major New York exhibition hall, hired out for various displays and fairs. This watercolor shows the annual exhibit (about 1845) of the American Institute, an organization which promoted advancement in commerce, agriculture and the arts.

The Garden and Theater was twice rebuilt after fires in 1846 and 1872. Theater fires caused fearful losses in New York — King's 1893 *Handbook of New York City* records thirty-seven theaters burned during the preceding century. Stringent building laws aimed at providing for fire protection in places of public assembly were finally passed in 1887.

THE GERMAN WINTER GARDEN.   Many private gathering places in New York offered special amusement in the foreign traditions of some of the city's residents. Partly to circumvent Sunday blue laws, a number of German beer gardens were established where Sabbath "Sacred Concerts" were held, and beer, radishes, cheese and Strauss waltzes could be enjoyed after payment of a small admission fee. The police apparently overlooked these early speakeasies, which were — behind plain facades — some of New York's most charming and elaborate meeting rooms. This watercolor shows the German Winter Garden which once stood at 45 Bowery. It was built around 1855, and the dome was one of the earliest made with cast-iron rib framing.

ATLANTIC GARDEN. Another celebrated German beer hall was Atlantic Garden, at 50 Bowery, between Bayard and Canal Streets, across the street from the German Winter Garden and just north of the Thalia Theater (see page 76). This engraving from *Harper's Magazine* shows the festivities on the occasion of the capitulation of Sedan to Germany, September 10, 1870. By this time, the most prominent German gathering place, Terrace Garden, had been established on 58th Street near Lexington Avenue. It had followed the German population over toward Yorkville, as the Bowery area was becoming run down. Terrace Garden was demolished in 1927. The last available view of the vanished Atlantic Garden is a 1922 photo owned by the New-York Historical Society, which shows this room to have turned dingy, though still as imposing as it seems below.

1

THE GARDEN AT MADISON SQUARE. The site of the first Madison Square Garden was an entire block bounded by Madison and Fourth Avenues and 26th and 27th Streets. In 1873 it held a performing arena adapted from railroad sheds which P. T. Barnum leased from Commodore Vanderbilt (1, center). It was originally known as the Great Roman Hippodrome, then as Gilmore's Garden (after the new leaseholder), and finally as Madison Square Garden when William H. Vanderbilt repossessed it in 1879. Pugilism, legal for the first time in New York, was the Garden's lucrative mainstay. The arena was in one of the city's most fashionable areas; it was across the park from the Fifth Avenue

2

Hotel (see page 71), and just north of the former Leonard Jerome mansion (1 and 2, right — the balconies are now gone but the building has become a designated Landmark).

The National Horse Show Association, formed in 1883, secured the property with the aid of J. P. Morgan. On the site they planned an elegant new home for the annual horse show, and held an architectural competition which was won by McKim, Mead and White. Stanford White became deeply engrossed in the project. He successfully argued for the completion of all aspects of his design, including a theater, a restaurant, a concert hall, a roof garden, a tower to be the second highest structure in the city, and arcades

3   4

which covered the sidewalks so the building would seem even closer to Madison Square Park. It was constructed as White had hoped (2) — of yellow brick and Pompeian white terra cotta, with an interior painted pink with cream-colored iron arched trusses (3). Augustus Saint-Gaudens provided a nude statute of Diana to top the spire, which became famous in its own right.

On June 16, 1890, the Garden opened its doors to 17,000 people, and as the contemporary press noted, it joined the Metropolitan Opera House and Carnegie Hall as one of the city's principal places of amusement. In magnitude, the Garden was the most important of the three. White took personal responsibility for its beauty, its critical success, and, ultimately, the blame for its financial failure. The Garden absorbed him even after completion. For the Columbian Quatercentenary in 1892 he made New York streets a carnival of lights with Edison's new incandescent bulbs, and Madison Square Garden, its tower spectacularly lit at night, was a big part of the show (4).

White was shot to death in the roof garden in 1906 by a deranged Pittsburgh millionaire (see page 233), and in the succeeding years his beloved Garden succumbed to foreclosure by the New York Life Insurance Company. It was at last demolished in 1925, the final lessee making no attempt to save it, though he managed to raise six million dollars for the construction of a new Garden away from Madison Square.

TAMMANY HALL. The New York Tammany Society was founded in 1789, growing out of the earlier Sons of Liberty. Like other Tammany organizations in other states it was named after Tamanend, Indian chief of the Delawares, and many of its observances and titles were borrowed from the Indians. In New York Aaron Burr was instrumental in setting up Tammany as a political power. The tiger, its famous symbol, was contributed by Mayor "Boss" Tweed.

The Society had four Wigwams in its history. Its famous second home was on Park Row and Frankfort Street, which was taken over by *The Sun* when Tammany moved to a new building in 1868. This one went up on the north side of 14th Street, between Third Avenue and Irving Place (2), next to the original Academy of Music (see page 79). Tony Pastor's Theater, a small variety house, operated within Tammany Hall from about 1877.

1

2

A color lithograph of the main hall shows an "Interior View of Tammany Hall Decorated for the National Convention, July 4th 1888" (1). This splendid room was demolished, along with the rest of the block, to make way for Consolidated Edison's office building. A new Tammany Hall was built on 17th Street and Fourth Avenue in 1929, but it is now a trade union hall. Tammany had long since become a euphemism for political bossism, and the "Society of Tammany or Columbian Order," which showed immigrants how to vote, elected Negro Aldermen, and organized candidates for Labor, today survives only in name.

1

RESTAURANTS.   Since restaurants usually occupy rented quarters, they are frequently the most short-lived of those private gathering places open to the public. Their impermanence may be due as often to gastronomic decline as to expiring leases. Architecturally, few can afford to create a complete milieu — it can only be a case of a new shop interior which changes scenery from the pharmacy that may have been there before, as a shoe repair shop might change it again later on. One such example was the vanished Broadmoor Restaurant, in a building on East 41st Street. Its interior (1) was designed by Ely Jacques Kahn. The decoration, characteristic of the '30s, appears to have been appropriately easy to paint over.

3

2

Some of the few New York restaurants actually run in homes of their own were among the most beloved and memorable. The Dining Room at Pennsylvania Station (2) was in a magnificent hall designed for it, and the Claremont Inn (3), converted from a country house before the Civil War, was a popular objective for excursions. The Inn was on Riverside Drive just north of Grant's Tomb until it was burned and demolished by the city in 1951.

Probably the most famous New York restaurant was Delmonico's. It started on William Street in the 1820s, and after nine moves arrived at the northeast corner of Fifth Avenue and 44th Street, in a building designed by James Brown Lord (4). The wrought-iron covered doors were opened in 1897, and closed forever in 1923 when the many dining rooms, ballrooms, supper-rooms and "bachelor apartments" were slated for destruction. Sherry's, Delmonico's great rival, had closed four years earlier for similar reasons, a victim — as Louis Sherry put it   of "Prohibition and war-born Bolshevism."

While it was a little harder to work out what could be done about Bolshevism, the end of Prohibition saw the old Central Park Casino glorified by Joseph Urban. The Black and Gold Room (5) was one of the rooms he redecorated in 1933, only a few years before the city tore down the entire building.

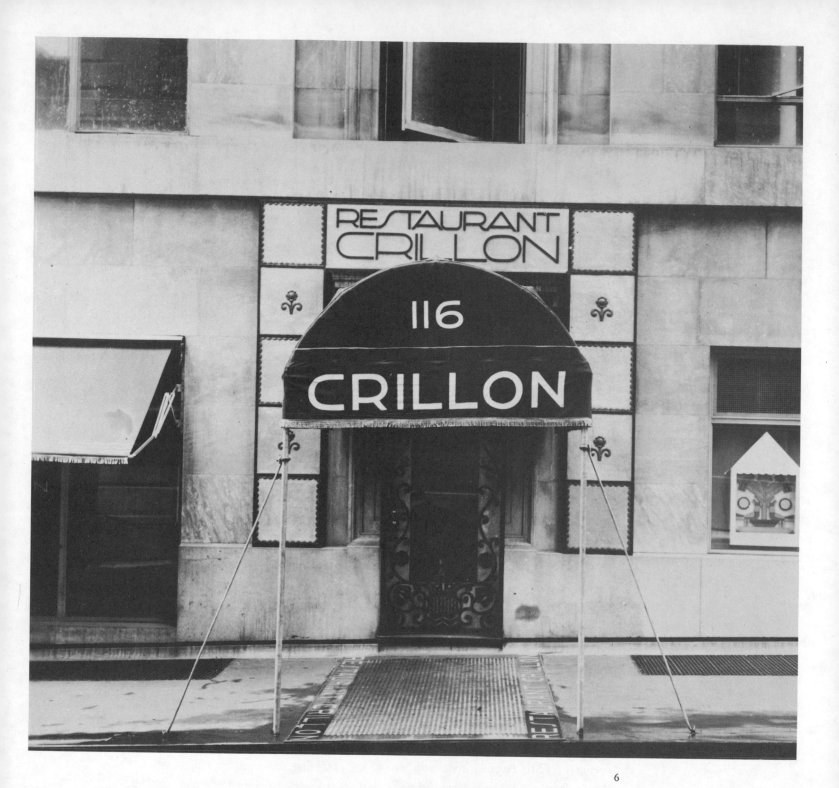

New York dining and drinking places have often had their own special design language, including the familiar covered-wagon canopy (6), and the long mahogany bar. The canopies remain, if not at the Crillon on 48th Street then at a thousand other restaurants all over the city; but many of the old zinc-and-mahogany-and-cut-glass taverns that once lined Sixth Avenue and Third Avenue have been altered beyond recognition, or have vanished for good.

CANFIELD'S GAMBLING HOUSE. Richard Canfield, who had been a nightclerk in a Union Square hotel in the 1870s, later moved uptown to become proprietor of his own gaming establishment at 5 East 44th Street. Canfield's Gambling House was infamously attractive to society layabouts. On one night in 1902, Reginald Claypoole Vanderbilt — still an undergraduate at Yale — reportedly dropped $70,000 at a session in one of the gaming rooms, perhaps this one.

Canfield's was the only prominent New York example of the casino life legally accessible in Europe, and there were many who loved the place. The imposing interiors survived until the late 1920s when the site was taken over for an office building.

HOTELS.   Many prominent New York hotels had disappeared even before the old Waldorf-Astoria was built. In Revolutionary times there were Bunker's, the Washington Tavern, Burn's and the Tontine Coffee Houses. In the 19th century, among the famous hotels which vanished were the St. Nicholas, Metropolitan, New York, Victoria, St. James, and the Brunswick on Fifth Avenue. Unlike most real estate redevelopment, these early hotels were frequently victims of actual obsolescence. Once prime lodgings, they gave way to a new standard of accommodation.

Hotels were originally inns which attempted only to provide satisfactory food and comfortable shelter for travelers. But starting with the construction of the Brunswick, luxury and elegance began to be made

1 2   3

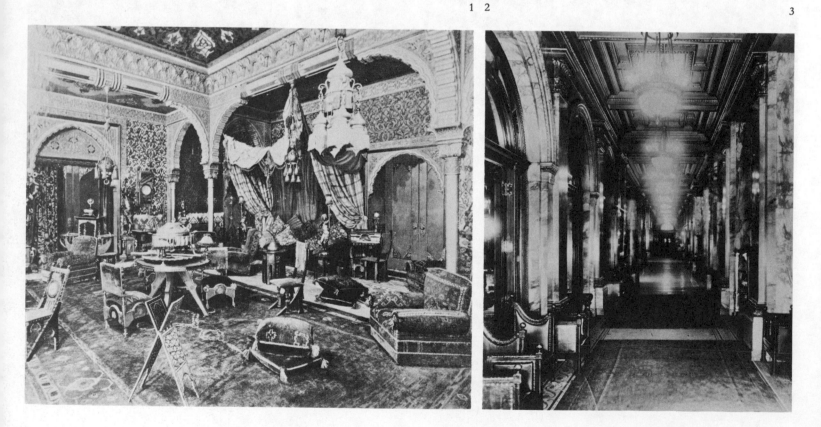

part of New York hotels as well. Because enough people could afford it and because fashionable New York society was making its own rules, the hotels started to purvey not only extremely comfortable quarters, but also undisputed social dignity. The new New York hotels were built to be homes for the quality, while elegant European hotels of the same period were still the rather disreputable transient places of Feydeau farces. Prosperous New Yorkers found that they did not need to maintain town residences if social standing was equally assured at certain hotels. To make way for this assurance, hotels that could not be transformed from mere public inns either went into decline or were discarded. The new hotels, besides providing such modern comforts as central heating, also offered shops and galleries, ballrooms, Royal Suites, and lecture halls. It became more common to take meals at a hotel under that lately rediscovered idea called the American Plan. In his 1899 book *The New Metropolis*, E. I. Zeisloft found that "People come to these colossal buildings, cities in themselves, not only for short stays, but for months at a time."

4

The Waldorf-Astoria was the most famous hotel to meet these transformed standards. The Waldorf part (3, left) was built in 1893 by William Waldorf Astor; then the rest of it, the Astoria (3, center and right), was added in 1895–97 by his aunt. Henry J. Hardenbergh was the architect. Dozens of the rooms and halls were at the disposal of the general public, including the Turkish Salon (1), where coffee was served by a genuine Turk and a boy assistant. Some were accessible by such grand galleries as Peacock Alley (2). Zeisloft marveled that "The poorest man living in or visiting New York, provided he is well dressed, may sit about these corridors night after night, spending never a cent, speaking to no one, and he will be allowed to stay."

The old Waldorf-Astoria met its end in a typical New York way: since the entire block was already under one ownership, it was cheaper for the builders of the future Empire State Building to buy it than to try to acquire nearby property piecemeal. One of the city's most valuable buildings consequently was demolished in 1929.

5

Splendor and elegance were characteristic not only of Manhattan hotels. Brooklyn had two on Coney Island, when that part of Brooklyn was still a long day's trip away from downtown New York. One of them was the Oriental, and the other the Manhattan Beach Hotel (4). The Manhattan Beach was really a resort hotel, only open during the summer season. Its electrically illuminated advertising sign at 23rd Street and Broadway, "Swept

7

by Ocean Breezes," was for a while a great New York curiosity. The Grand View Hotel (5), which once stood in the Fort Hamilton section of Brooklyn, was undoubtedly a less luxurious place, despite its splendid ornamented galleries. The grand view referred to was presumably the Narrows and the Lower Bay.

As the Grand View was built in a timber style characteristic of its probable construction date in the '70s, the Park Avenue Hotel by John Kellum (6), on 33rd Street in Manhattan, had a cast-iron facade of the same decade. Originally established by the merchant prince A. T. Stewart in 1878 as a home for working women, it became a luxury hotel when strict house rules made the first scheme a failure. It was torn down in 1927. The Murray Hill Hotel (7), nearby at Park Avenue between 40th and 41st Streets, was a seven-story building with two pointed corner towers and over 500 rooms. Its site now holds an office building.

8

The beginning of the fashion for living in the country and boarding in town probably began with the opening of the Astor House (8) in 1836, designed by Isaiah Rogers and sensational for its interior plumbing on all floors. It stood on Broadway between Vesey and Barclay Streets, a square building with a square courtyard inside until part of it was demolished in 1913, the rest following in 1926. Meanwhile the fashionable hotel district had long since shifted from lower Broadway. For a while it centered on the Madison Square area, where the Fifth Avenue Hotel stood (9) on Fifth Avenue between 23rd and 24th Streets, built 1856–58 with the first New York hotel elevator by William Washburn, architect. During the Columbian Quatercentenary, *The Times* of London said that no hostelry in the world had ever entertained so many distinguished people. It was demolished in 1908, only sixteen years later, for by

9

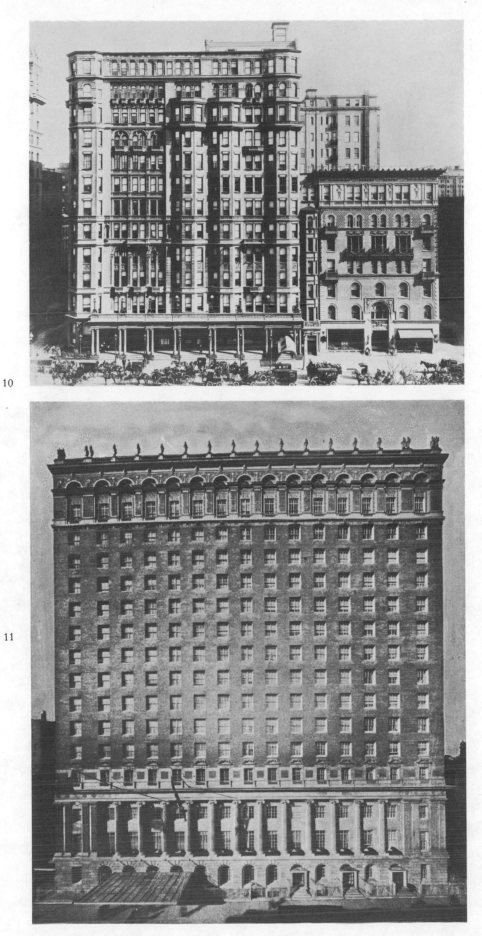

10

11

12

13

14

then the best neighborhoods — and best hotels — were far uptown. One of these was the Savoy (10), on the east side of the Plaza at 59th Street, built in 1890–92 after designs by Ralph S. Townsend. This hotel and the Bolkenhayn Apartments next to it were torn down in 1926 to make way for the grander Savoy-Plaza Hotel (see page 25).

There are those who believe that the finest of all New York hotels was the Ritz-Carlton (11), by Warren & Wetmore, architects of the new Grand Central Terminal. The Ritz-Carlton, on Madison Avenue and 46th Street, reached its fashionable heyday at about the time of the First World War. Its ballrooms and lobbies (12, 13), and some say its service and general *ambiance*, were better than those furnished later elsewhere at the Ritz Tower. The Ritz-Carlton was razed in 1951 to provide a site for an office building.

Hotels were often engulfed by the prosperity they created. The Buckingham (14), on Fifth Avenue between 49th and 50th Streets, found itself a perfect location when it was built in the 1870s, and the fashionable district moved up around it. But ultimately the site proved too perfect, since it became valuable enough to be bought up for the construction of a department store.

New York hotel building now appears to have gone through two complete cycles — first the era of comfortable city inns, typified by the Brevoort and the old Fifth Avenue hotels; then the period of luxurious elegance of which the old Waldorf-Astoria and the Ritz-Carlton were examples. The hotels of the second cycle, by setting a new standard, did much to undermine the prosperity of the first. A third cycle of New York hotel building has now begun, based on the idea of standardized mass accommodation. However, the tourist and convention trade currently being sought is not the same as the clientele still being provided for by the remaining accommodations of the second cycle. It would be sad for New York if the newest hotels were permitted to eradicate the last of the luxury palaces.

1

THEATERS. Of all the institutions associated with civic advance, theaters have probably been the most highly esteemed. From the mid-18th century, when theaters were instruments for the enhancement of society and fashion, to the mid-20th century, when they are supposed to be vessels of culture, new theaters have been credited as being the fairest architectural examples of the splendor and spirit of the community. Even privately-owned theaters, operated for profit, have been hailed as municipal improvements when built, when in fact — as has frequently occurred in New York — they may have supplanted better buildings. Change has often been more characteristic than improvement, though fire was frequently to blame. The rapid rate of new theater building in New York has far outstripped advancements in theater technology. It would seem that new theaters, like a woman's annual spring fashions, are primarily meant to support ideas of freshness, reaffirmation and vitality. This being so, it is no wonder that the old gowns are pushed to the back of the closet.

3

A few wholly modern New York theaters have already vanished. The Center Theater in Rockefeller Center (1, 2), built as recently as 1932 by the architects Reinhard & Hofmeister, Corbett Harrison & MacMurray, and Hood & Fouilhoux, had an auditorium (2) quite as good if somewhat less stunning than their nearby Radio City Music Hall. And some of the interior design, such as Edward Steichen's photo mural in the Men's Smoking Room (1), far surpassed any of the callow artwork which survives at Rockefeller Center. But the Center Theater has now been renovated out of existence — filled in with levels of office floors — because its theatrical uses, even for television work, were not as profitable as its potential use as offices.

There is some doubt about the date of the earliest theatrical performance in New York City. Probably there was no such thing under the Dutch. The first record of the appearance of a professional actor was in 1730, during the British colonial administration. In 1750 an acting company arrived from London and hired a hall in Nassau Street for their performances of *Richard III*. After a five-month run with two performances a week the company disbanded, but the hall was used again, and was called the Nassau Street Theater.

4

In 1753 it was rebuilt by the Hallam family, who operated it until the following year. It was converted into a church in 1758. Three years later the Chapel Street Theater was built, only to be destroyed in 1764 by a mob unsympathetic to that form of amusement. Despite this, the John Street Theater — on John Street close to Broadway — opened in 1767, survived through the Revolution as the sometime Theater Royal, and later often entertained George Washington when New York was the Federal capital. The John Street was converted into a carriage factory in 1798.

The first New York theater with architectural and cultural pretensions was the Park Theater, on Park Row (3). The architects were Joseph and Charles Mangin, Joseph later collaborating in the design of City Hall across the street. The theater, begun in 1795, opened in 1798 with a performance of *As You Like It*. It burned down in 1820, was rebuilt, then burned down again in 1848, to be replaced by commercial buildings. Meanwhile a number of rivals had appeared: the Water Street Theater, the Grove Street Theater, Vauxhall Gardens, the New Olympic, and the Anthony Street Theater, where Edmund Kean made his New York debut in 1820. The most serious rival to the Park

was the Chatham Garden Theater (4), erected in 1824 (architect unknown). It subsequently changed its name to Blanchard's Amphitheater, since it was mostly devoted to comedy and light opera. The Park continued to hold on to its fashionable audience, however, and the unprofitable Chatham Garden was converted out of existence in 1832. By that time Niblo's Garden and Theater had been built (see page 47), a popular place with a long life in its several incarnations. In 1866 it was the scene of the first run of *The Black Crook*, the ancestor of modern musicals.

The Bowery Theater, at 46 Bowery, was designed by Ithiel Town and opened in 1826 as the New-York Theater. Early Living Newspaper-type productions were staged there; one in 1859, two weeks after the execution of John Brown, was called *The Insurrection, or Kansas and Harper's Ferry*. The Bowery was gutted by fire four times, but each time the exterior, considered a marvel of architectural beauty, remained safe. In 1879 it was rechristened the Thalia, and its columniated facade was later partially hidden by the Third Avenue El (6). Along with the Castle Garden theater (see page 96) it was considered one of the two great theatrical landmarks of old New York — until demolished in the early 20th century.

While the Nassau Street and Chatham Garden theaters were converted into churches, A. T. Stewart's Broadway Athenaeum (5) was a theater made from a church, remodeled in 1865 by J. H. Hackett. It operated under various managers as Daly's New Fifth-Avenue Theater, Fox's Broadway Theater, The Globe, and finally as the New Théâtre Comique when it was run by Harrigan & Hart. It stood at 728–30 Broadway opposite Waverly Place until it burned down in 1884.

The Théâtre Français opened in 1866 on 14th Street, west of Sixth Avenue. After some French-language productions it changed management and names several times (11). The street facade was unique. Its double portico, which provided protection for the audience at both lobby and gallery levels, was a handsome and distinguishing feature, even after it had been marred by fire escapes (the canopy over the sidewalk — less electric signs — appears to have been there from the start). As the Civic Repertory, it was run by Eva Le Gallienne from 1926 until 1932, devoted mainly to modern classic dramas. When the Repertory's subsidy gave out, the enterprise was discontinued and the building was ultimately demolished.

Other historically important downtown theaters were Tripler Hall and Wallack's. Tripler Hall, on Broadway opposite Bond Street, was built to serve for Jenny Lind's American debut (which, however, took place at Castle Garden instead, because Tripler Hall was not finished). It was later known as the New-York Theater, the Metropolitan Opera-House, Laura Keene's Varieties, and the Winter Garden,

suffering some fires between transformations. As the Winter Garden it
burned to the ground in 1867. The famous Wallack's, the second theater of
that name to be run by the Wallack family, was on Broadway and 13th Street.
It opened in 1861 and had great popularity for twenty years because of the management's high production standards. In 1881 the name was changed to the
Germania, and in 1883 it became called the Star. It was later pulled down, but
by this time the Bowery Era of the New York stage had long since ended.
Italian opera was first heard in America at the Park Theater on November 29,
1825. The opera was *The Barber of Seville*. Lorenzo da Ponte, Mozart's
great librettist (exiled from Venice and teaching at Columbia) promoted the
first New York building devoted to opera — the 1833 Italian Opera House,
at the southwest corner of Leonard and Church Streets. But the company's
failure caused the building to be soon used as a playhouse. The same fate befell

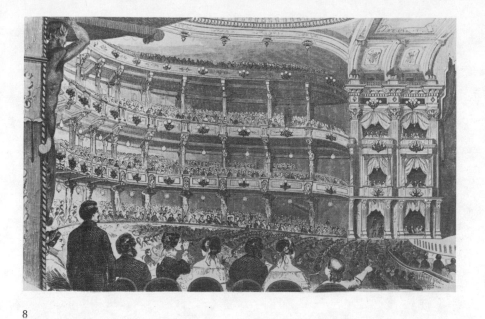

8

Palmo's Opera House which opened in 1844. The Astor Place Opera House, built by private subscription, opened in 1847 with *Ernani*. A year later it too became a playhouse, the scene of the Astor Place Riot in 1849 in which over twenty people were killed. In this incident Forrest, an American tragedian, was favored against his great English rival, Macready. Triggered by a performance in which Forrest put heavy double meaning into Macbeth's Act V, Scene 3, line, "What rhubarb, senna, or what purgative drug, would scour these English hence?" the audience stopped the drama with cheering, and the uproar began. The Academy of Music, at the northeast corner of 14th Street and Irving Place, was the first opera house at which opera remained popular. It was built in 1854 (7), burned down in 1866, and was rebuilt in 1868. The interior view (8), from *Ballou's Pictorial Drawing-Room Companion*, is described in the text: "The prevailing color is white, relieved by gold and crimson velvet. Let the reader look upon the engraving, and imagine every line in the picture to be a gold stripe, with the brilliant effect of a thousand gas lights shining thereupon, the private and stage boxes upholstered in the richest manner — and he may perhaps form some faint conception of the magnificent *ensemble* of this interior. Spacious and commodious, it is admirably adapted for seeing and hearing. The seats are all single, and constructed on the plan of those in the Boston and European theaters, the seat being so hinged that when the sitter rises it folds up against the back, allowing 'ample room and verge enough' to move about and make one's exit without inconvenience. The house will seat about four thousand comfortably." The opening of the Metropolitan Opera House in 1883 (see page 206), built by a corporation consisting largely of people who were unable to get boxes at the Academy of Music, put the Academy out of fashion. It was sold, altered for straight plays, and ultimately replaced by an office building.

After the 1866 fire at the Academy of Music, Samuel N. Pike of Cincinnati built an opera house in New York which opened in 1868. Pike's Opera House, at the northwest corner of Eighth Avenue and 23rd Street, was sold to Jim Fisk and Jay Gould the following year, and renamed the Grand Opera House (9, 10). It finally became a movie theater and survived until recently.

Among other New York operatic ventures, perhaps the best remembered were launched by Oscar Hammerstein at two separate Manhattan Opera Houses, built in 1892 and 1910. Both efforts were short-lived.

In 1909 the elegant New Theater was opened at Central Park West and 62nd Street (12), designed by Carrère and Hastings. The monumental lobby (13) and auditorium (14), reminiscent in style of the same

9

10

11

architects' New York Public Library, became the home in 1913–15 of yet another effort to rival the Met. The theater was renamed the Century Opera House. Later it was demolished to make way for the Century Apartments.

Until very recently, when thrust stages and arena theaters came back into vogue, there were only three basic types of theater built in modern times, and New York had some outstanding representatives of all three. There was the playhouse, with a somewhat narrow proscenium and overhanging balconies; the opera house, with a wider stage, bigger audience capacity and shallow galleries of boxes; and, created in the 20th century, the movie house.

New York movie houses began to depart from the scope of the nickelodeon in 1912 when Adolph Zukor imported the four-reel picture *Queen Elizabeth*. Its financial success led to *Quo Vadis*, an eight-reeler, which was shown at the Astor Theater for twenty-two consecutive weeks in 1913 at the unheard-of top price of one dollar. The Astor was a playhouse. The need for a more suitable theater was evident, and the following year Mitchell and Moe Mark from Buffalo opened the Strand Theater on the northwest

corner of Broadway and 47th Street, employing architect Thomas W. Lamb and, as project manager, an imaginative thirty-one-year-old who had recently been making a vast commercial success out of the Regent, a big purpose-designed movie house on 116th Street. His name was Samuel L. Rothafel, called "Roxy" because that had been his nickname when he briefly played semi-pro baseball. The story of Roxy's and others' achievements in turning the nickelodeon into a new building type, the movie palace — one of the greatest of which would be named after Roxy — is told on pages 214–16.

In a phenomenal few years after the opening of the Strand, movie palaces began erupting in midtown New York. While they were built in other cities, too, the New York movie palaces' booking records ("four smash weeks at the Roxy") became potent sales statistics to regional exhibitors when films had a

closely analyzed first run in New York before national release. Motion picture companies quickly moved to own or control the vast film theaters, which for most of their brief lives operated as barely profitable introductory presentation houses. The Depression checked the building of any more venues that would frequently show losses, but the real cause of their decline was the success of Vitagraph sound after 1927, when live orchestral music became redundant. Additionally, as double features started being shown in local film theaters, accompanying stage shows lost importance as an audience draw.

But even as the huge, full-stage-equipped midtown movie palaces began their commercial decline, it remained desirable for regional and neighborhood film theaters to have large auditoriums and luxury-fantasy appointments. One of the most exciting in New York was Loew's 72nd Street, opened in 1932

15

16

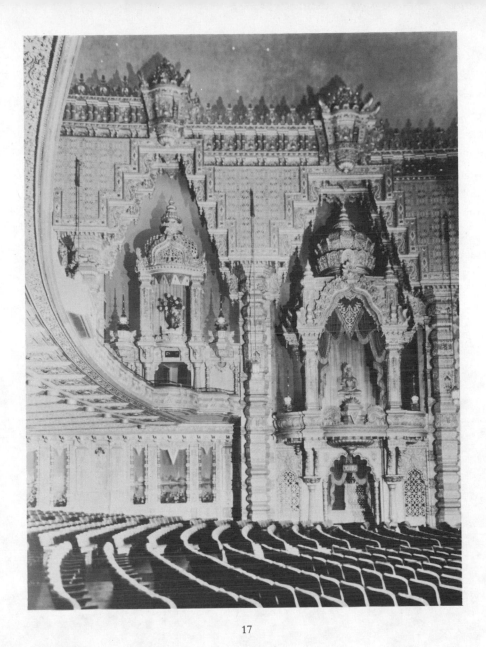

17

(the Depression actually encouraged attendance at local theaters) and demolished in 1961. The lobby (15), the mezzanine promenade (16) and the auditorium (17) were gorgeously decorated with gilded forms slightly reminiscent of Angkor Wat or perhaps an even more remote inspiration — another setting for the Big Screenplay and the recherché pleasures of the world. The architect of Loew's 72nd Street was the Strand's Thomas Lamb, working with John Eberson as decorator. The story of Eberson, an especially talented and imaginative scenographic designer, is told further on page 216.

As the most fashionable hotels, restaurants and residential addresses had done, playhouses also moved uptown. "The legitimate theater" found its new home "on Broadway," a west side area that began at about 34th Street and later centered itself at about 45th Street. Oscar Hammerstein built the opulent Olympia Theater on the east side of Broadway between 44th and 45th Streets. It was a vast entertainment palace which contained a concert hall, theater, roof garden and oriental cafe, and was an almost instant financial disaster. It then changed its name to the Lyric. Parts of the virtually unrecognizable carcass of the building survive in the Criterion Theater.

The Casino Theater (18), "one of the picturesque buildings of New-York City," according to King's 1893 *Handbook of New York*, was on the southeast corner of Broadway and 39th Street, "a fine illustration of the Arabesque or Moorish style of architecture." The Casino was built in 1882 to be a concert hall but usually played comic opera. The auditorium and roof garden were Arabesque or Moorish as well, fully detailed by Kimball & Wisedell, the architects. The Shuberts took over the house in 1902. It suffered a fire in 1905, but the famous theater survived until 1930. The Fulton Theater on West 46th Street (19), never destroyed but substantially altered as the present Helen Hayes Theater, was similarly designed for external appearance and street effect. It opened in 1911 as a theater-restaurant featuring the "Folies Bérgère." The Earl Carroll Theater, like the Ziegfeld on Sixth Avenue (see page 205), was devised to suit an audience who came to see girls glorified in ostrich feathers. The lobby ticket counter (20), once just inside its Broadway entrance, was a perfect model of the now-lost Broadway called the Great White Way.

18   19

20

CIVIC ARCHITECTURE.

Buildings highly adapted to use are a recent development, coming from the modern idea that architectural form ought to be determined by the activities within. Architects speak of "building types" when similar interior activities make buildings resemble each other. Contemporary libraries resemble other libraries, not banks or schools.

But when architecture first became a fit subject for scholarship, distinctions according to building type were not thought to be particularly important — partly because activities were less specialized, partly because the architects lacked aesthetic license to express differences. From the Renaissance almost to the present, architectural historians treated buildings as formal expressions of primarily social or environmental import. Buildings were first categorized as either religious or secular. After that, the broad architectural subdivisions were Military, Civil and Domestic. This followed the idea that the most important consideration determining the appearance of a building was whether it was predominantly public or private. While a library, a bank and a school — being all public buildings — could look much alike, it was naturally important to make fine distinctions among palaces.

Most of New York's civic architecture was built primarily to be Civil Architecture. The buildings are not straightforward types so much as they are public buildings, designed to be well-mannered elements of a general municipal environment. In this sense, such things as deliberate monumentality, use of ornament, and eclectic formal styles should be seen not as shallow "facade architecture" but as aspects of a quite different aesthetic — attempts at concordant building in the public view. The fact that New York, like most cities, has had a predominance of such buildings may explain something about the agreeable if unremarkable overall character they have provided, and the feeling of loss and disruption in the city when they vanish.

The Croton Reservoir, Fifth Avenue from 40th to 42nd Streets, built 1839–43 with James Renwick employed as building Clerk-of-the-Works. The granite walls were forty-four and a half feet high. The reservoir was widely held, along with the first Tombs Prison, to be one of the two finest examples of "Egyptian architecture" in the country. People could parade around the rim by day or night for a bird's-eye view of the city. It was demolished in 1899–1900 to make way for the New York Public Library.

FEDERAL HALL.   From both an architectural and a historical point of view, Federal Hall might well have been the greatest national landmark had it survived. It stood on the northeast corner of Wall and Nassau Streets, on a site now occupied by the old Sub-Treasury building. Federal Hall was first built in 1699 as a new city hall. In 1788–89 it was substantially altered by Major Pierre Charles L'Enfant, one of Lafayette's officers — the same man who later did the plan of Washington, D.C. The remodeled Hall, shown in this print, had a facade much like Inigo Jones's unexecuted London design of 1617 for the Star Chamber. Yet when the remodeling was complete, it was taken as a polemic of French taste and became the beginning of the Federal style that flourished with Jefferson's approval and encouragement. The Hall was the scene of the first Congress after the Constitution, of Washington's election as President, and of his inauguration on April 30, 1789, which took place on the balcony. As he kissed the Bible after taking the oath of office, a flag was shown at the cupola to signal the firing of all the guns at the Battery and the ringing of all the bells in the city. When Congress transferred to Philadelphia, Federal Hall once again became City Hall, which it remained until the present city hall was completed in 1812.

GOVERNMENT HOUSE. In New York, Washington had lived in borrowed houses on Cherry Street and Broadway. An opportunity for building an official residence presented itself in 1789 when the state legislature decided upon the destruction of old Fort Amsterdam, leaving the site clear for a new public building. With its Ionic porch and decorated windows, Government House (attributed to James Robinson) was rather more Georgian than Federalist in character. It became the New York governor's mansion when the federal government moved away in August, 1790. After 1798 it was used as a hotel, as government offices, and as a custom house. The state tried to sell the property to New York City in May, 1812, but since the proposed transaction stipulated that the land could not be resold for private purposes, the city council took no interest, while that same month rapaciously ordering the sale at auction of Federal Hall, which the purchaser immediately tore down. The state amended its Government House offer in 1813, arranging its sale subject only to the soon-to-expire public lease. The city then bought it, and in 1815 bagged its profit by selling off the property in seven parcels. Government House was burned and demolished.

FIRE AND SHOT TOWERS.   In the days of wood and masonry construction fire was the greatest civic problem, and the City of New York built a number of towers to serve as fire watch and alarm stations. One of these was shown in a contemporary magazine (1). According to the description: "This curious structure is situated in 33rd Street [the picture caption says 43rd Street], near its junction with Ninth Avenue. It was erected in 1851, by Messrs. Bogardus & Hoppin, builders in iron . . . One of the most notable points in the construction of this tower, was the drilling of the rock for the insertion of . . . anchorage shafts. The drilling was accomplished by means of machinery invented for the purpose. The lower part of the cavities drilled are larger than at the surface, so that the lower ends of the shafts, each being split, are, by the ingenious insertion of a wedge, made to spread, and are thus immovably imbedded in the rock. The cost of the tower was $6,000 . . . The Corporation of New York are now erecting a second fire tower, similar to the above, near the corner of Macdougal and Spring Streets." The

1

2

usefulness of fire towers was largely supplanted by a telegraph alarm system established in the late 1850s and a paid New York Fire Department in 1865.

James Bogardus, the builder of the fire tower shown, was a manufacturer of grinding machinery, and an inventor and popularizer of a complete cast-iron building system (see page 166). Among his other works were shot towers (2) — not really civic, except in an ornamental sense (though they were sometimes used for fire watch stations). Gunshot was made by splashing molten lead through screens at the top of a tower. The droplets then cooled into spheres as they fell through the air. Bogardus's shot towers, of which two were built in the 1850s in New York, were cast iron load-bearing structures with masonry infilling, the first true skeleton structures in the modern world. One at 63–65 Centre Street survived until 1908 (3), when it was torn down during subway construction.

3

ST. LUKE'S HOSPITAL. Many of New York's largest hospitals are private institutions. St. Luke's, the leading Protestant Episcopal hospital, was founded on a site on West 54th Street and Fifth Avenue by the Reverend William A. Muhlenberg in 1854; John W. Ketch, architect. All the parts of the building in the photograph — including the chapel between the two towers — were open in 1858 on their large grassy plot. But since hospitals notoriously require ever-improving facilities and an expanding plant, the present site of St. Luke's on Morningside Drive was chosen, and competition-winner Ernest Flagg began supervising construction of the new buildings in 1893. In 1896 the painted brick institution on Fifth Avenue was demolished.

TOMPKINS MARKET ARMORY.   The Seventh Regiment, which gained some prominent friends after the Astor Place Riot, was unified under one roof in 1860 in the Tompkins Market Armory. This was a handsome structure on the east side of the Bowery between 6th and 7th Streets, the first building erected by New York City with special facilities for an individual military unit. Within the iron frame, the first floor was a market, the second floor Company rooms, and the third floor (under an arched vault, an earlier roof structure than the timber trusses shown in this 1911 demolition photograph) was the drill room. The building's multiple use was an outstanding idea for maintaining the property's economy; but the Regiment moved to its own armory on Park Avenue in 1880 (see page 203).

CASTLE GARDEN: THE AQUARIUM. The Battery was originally an artillery position. It was supplemented about 1807 by the Southwest Battery, a fortification 300 feet offshore, later called Castle Clinton after being improved by John McComb, Jr. When the federal government took over Governor's Island for use as a military base in 1822, the Battery properties were ceded to New York. The city used the Battery as a promenade and parade ground. Across its connecting drawbridge, Castle Clinton was made into a public assembly room and renamed Castle Garden.

Beginning with the 1824 reception for the return of Lafayette to the United States, Castle Garden established itself as New York's most eminent civic hall. It was there that Barnum arranged Jenny Lind's fabulous American debut (1) on September 11, 1850. The building had outstanding qualities for diverse uses (2), and in 1896, after a term as the U.S. Immigrant Station, it accommodated the New York Aquarium. Landfill had meanwhile gradually absorbed the island into Battery Park (3).

After over fifty years of popularity, the Aquarium was unwisely closed and moved to far less accessible Coney Island. Since losing its use, the old building has been "restored" back to its presumed earliest condition, and is now called "Castle Clinton National Monument."

1

2

3

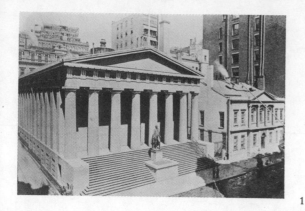

1

THE ASSAY OFFICE.　　This building was erected at 30 Wall Street in 1823 to be the New York branch of the Bank of the United States; Martin E. Thompson, architect. After the failure of that institution it served two other banks. It was bought by the government and made into a U.S. Assay Office, where gold and silver were refined and made into bullion from 1854 to 1912. Until demolished in 1915, it stood next to the Sub-Treasury building (1, left). The esteemed facade was re-erected in 1924 at the Metropolitan Museum.

2

1

COLUMBIA'S MIDTOWN CAMPUS. Columbia has existed on three sites. From 1754 to 1857 it was at Church Street and Park Place (as King's College and a Tory hotbed it had been disbanded during the Revolution). From 1857 it used some buildings in midtown near a legacy to Columbia from an alumnus, the Elgin Botanical Garden estate. The library, built in 1884, was on 49th Street (1, right), and at the corner of 50th Street and Madison was Hamilton Hall of 1880 (2) — "Collegiate Gothic" buildings by Charles C. Haight. The third site, on Morningside Heights, was acquired in 1892, and a few years later the midtown campus was abandoned.

2

FIREHOUSE.   In 1819 the New York volunteer fire brigades began to abandon buckets in favor of a great improvement in fire-fighting equipment — the hose. Since hoses had to be dried after use, the need for specially designed firehouses was an economically significant reason for the establishment of the municipal fire department. This classic firehouse, with hose drying tower, was on Park Avenue and 135th Street, until demolished to make way for the East River Drive.

COTTON EXCHANGE.   New York's strength as a financial capital is largely based on its exchanges, where stocks, bonds, and commodities are freely traded.   The Stock Exchange — said to have begun under a buttonwood tree — has expanded and moved several times, but the Cotton Exchange was organized only in 1871.   This building, designed for the Exchange by George B. Post, was completed in 1885 at William and Beaver Streets, where a new one now stands.   Besides providing a thirty-five foot high exchange room and a clubhouse, the Cotton Exchange adopted standards, settled disputes, and established commercial principles.   Within Post's bit of Chambord with the characteristic downtown-Manhattan corner entrance, cotton traders were first made to feel at home in New York.

THE PRODUCE EXCHANGE.   George B. Post's most noted work may have been the Western Union building (see page 162), but his most notable one was the Produce Exchange (1), finished in 1884 at Bowling Green on Beaver Street. The mammoth structure was faced with rich dark red brick, which later provided a striking contrast to the white stone building and sculpture of the Custom House (2). Terra cotta bas-reliefs on the Produce Exchange were of the produce traded within. The building had a true iron skeleton, finished a year before Jenney's Home Insurance building in Chicago. The main hall on the second floor (3) measured 220 by 144 feet, with heights of 47 feet to the ceiling and 60 feet to the skylight. The Produce Exchange, one of the best buildings in New York, was replaced after 1957 by one of the worst.

1

2

3

JAILS.   Historically, jails have been a great social convenience, and it was long considered to be of public benefit to put them on display. While the effectiveness of the cautionary lesson may be open to doubt, there is, as Piranesi knew, no question of the effectiveness of prisons in architectural expression. From Loches on the Loire to the Allegheny County Jail in Pittsburgh, jails have presented themselves to the world as sheer monuments — formal exhibition objects of massive geometrical masonry.

New York has had no buildings as terror-haunted as Loches or as awe-inspiring as Richardson's Pittsburgh jail, but the prisons built have nevertheless offered citizens some obvious expressionism. The first Tombs Prison (2), by architect John Haviland, was finished in 1838 on the filled-in Collect Pond; the choice of site was a nice symbolic touch, since a pre-Revolutionary gibbet stood on an island there. The name arose from its associations — although the neo-Egyptian architecture was more reminiscent of a temple than a tomb.

The Tombs gave way in 1897 to the new Tombs on the same site (3), a fortress which had 320 cells and two chapels. It was replaced about 1947 by the new Criminal Courts building at Leonard and Centre Streets.

The Jefferson Market Prison (1), at Greenwich Avenue and 10th Street, was a minor city prison used for temporary detention, and typical of other small jails attached to police courts. Its significance lies in the fact that the prison and courthouse (built 1874–77 by Frederick Clark Withers and Calvert Vaux), together with a market and firehouse, were probably New York's first comprehensive public building group, though not simultaneously planned. Everything except the courthouse and its clocktower was demolished in 1927 to make way for a new prison, the Women's House of Detention, which was itself demolished in the 1970s when the courthouse became a library. The idea of discipline as an architectural problem in penal fortification continues to erode.

1   2 3

1

THE CITY HALL POST OFFICE.   It may be only modern sophistication to think that the Post Office between Broadway and Park Row (1) was a handsome and vigorous building, because almost from the first it was considered a municipal eyesore. It became the city's main post office in 1875, when postal services moved from the old Middle Dutch Church building (see page 147). A. B. Mullett, the government architect, had done his best to see that the building had modern and adequate facilities — such as a pneumatic system that linked the building with other stations, and loading bays along one side which were afterward covered with canopies (4).

What was impressive about the building in a formal sense was its relentless fragmentation of architectural elements (2), dramatically superior even to the same architect's State, War and Navy Department

3

2

building in Washington, finished the same year. But its most compelling trait was the way the Post Office played against City Hall (3), a building of about the same volume. The Post Office served to enclose the south side of City Hall Park, and even the mistake of having the loading docks on the north side of the Post Office did not spoil the principle of the neat urban square. When Cass Gilbert's Woolworth Tower was built (3, tallest building), the Post Office not only made it seem taller, but it kept City Hall from appearing as an isolated dwarf.

Even though City Hall Park was somewhat extended after the Post Office was demolished in 1939, this urban scene was, on balance, much weakened by the new long view down Broadway and the sight of some clumsy highway engineering at the intersection where the Post Office had been.

THE MUSEUM OF MODERN ART, STAGE I.   The Museum, at 11 West 53rd Street, was a glistening intruder in 1939, when it shattered a block of brownstones with its crisp design and careful scale. New additions by Philip Johnson are in character, but not unified with the original street wall. The Museum has consequently lost the contrast with the street which was the explicit visual virtue of the building by Philip L. Goodwin and Edward D. Stone.

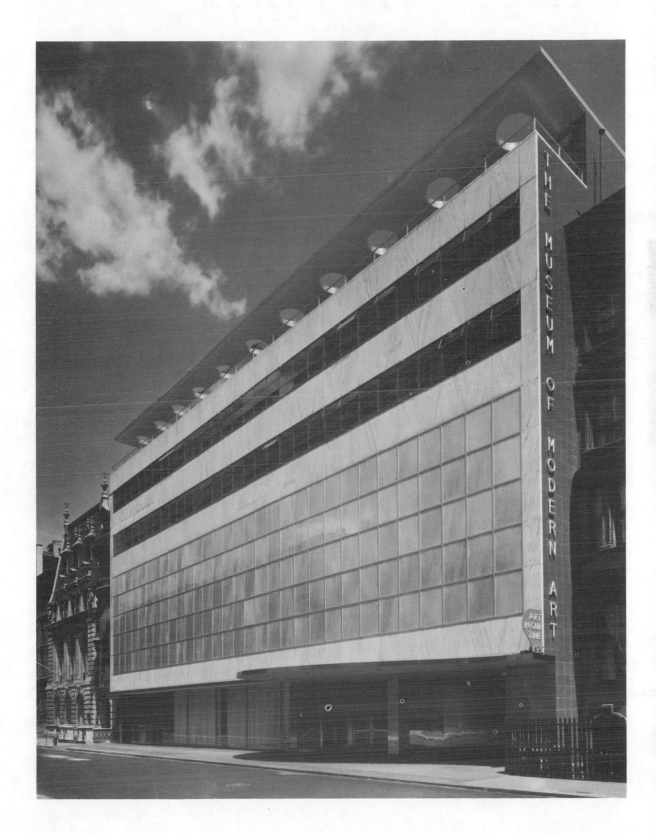

GREAT HOUSES.

Compared to other cities, a relatively large number of people in New York have been able to accumulate an enormous amount of wealth. During the 19th century there were fortunes to be made in a growing country, and in a growing city (with real estate still cheap) prestige could be bought. These mutually agreeable circumstances led to palace-building of a quantity without precedent in any city of the world. Most of the financiers, landlords, merchants and operators who amassed fortunes in the city built great houses. And even many entrepreneurs whose profits were made elsewhere built New York *Stadtpalasts* for their families. Within a scant three generations Manhattan changed from a mostly rural, certainly provincial city into an imperial capital. The great houses at first lined downtown streets, then midtown Fifth Avenue, and finally upper Fifth Avenue and avenues on the West Side.

Support for the mansions of the rich at first seems hardly an important civic responsibility. Yet the family palaces of the 19th century were unique New York elements, authentic manifestations of a time and place. Having created some fashionable streets, many great houses later became early victims of rising property values. Those that remain, particularly along Fifth Avenue, ought to be preserved — either to be turned over to institutions sympathetic to their character, or in the best examples (as the English National Trust has done to many houses) maintained intact with furnishings, and opened to the public.

House of Cornelius Vanderbilt II — the carriage entrance, facing the Plaza. The building was begun with the southern section in 1880 and was enlarged in 1894 at this northern end, after designs by George B. Post and certain details by Richard M. Hunt. The house had thirty servants. It was demolished in 1927 to make way for a department store. Only the north gates remain, re-erected in Central Park at 105th Street.

THE APTHORPE MANSION.　Charles Ward Apthorpe, a Colonial lawyer, built this house in about 1764 on his 200 acre farm on the Bloomingdale Road. The portico doorway opened into a hall the full depth of the house, large enough for a cotillion party. Walls, mantels and ceilings in all the main rooms were paneled in English brown oak: in an era of costly transportation, evidence of the owner's great wealth. The mansion was headquarters at different times for Clinton, Howe and Washington. It was later converted into a tavern, which stood near 91st Street and Columbus Avenue. The building was torn down in 1892 when a row of apartment houses was built on the site.

DORIC MANSION.   The Greek Revival and the Gothic Revival were individual modes of what has been called Romantic Classicism, an attitude where cultural ideals were symbolized by the inventive re-use of distant architectural forms. The vanished Anderson house on Throgs Neck, the Bronx, was built about 1830; probably by Josiah R. Brady, architect. To those inspired by classical culture, the Doric order used was primitive and wild. It was an early Greek figure, appropriate for an almost solitary landscape.

GOTHIC VILLA.   Alexander Jackson Davis, for a time a partner of Ithiel Town, was an architect who arrived in New York from Connecticut in the early 19th century. At first doing odd jobs in art — he made the drawing of the Doric Mansion on page 113 — he soon began to get a great deal of architectural work. As an example of one side of the double ideal of Romantic Classicism, nothing could be clearer than the house he did for W. C. H. Waddell, illustrated in 1844. Since the house — at the northwest corner of 37th Street and Fifth Avenue — was a suburban villa, it was appropriate for it to be casually Picturesque. The house was demolished in 1856 to make way for a church, which was in turn destroyed in 1938.

GREEK PALACE. The other side of the Romantic Classical ideal aimed at the Sublime, and many houses were designed like Greek temples, a fancy initiated in America by Thomas Jefferson and Benjamin Latrobe. A. J. Davis's house for the wealthy ship builder John Cox Stevens, now also lost, was a Corinthian-columned affair which was built about 1849 near Murray Street and West Broadway. Since it was a town house, it needed to be starched and lordly. Of it, the contemporary diarist Philip Hone wrote: "The Palais Bourbon in Paris, Buckingham Palace in London and the Sans Souci at [sic] Berlin are little grander than this residence of a simple citizen of our Republican city . . ."

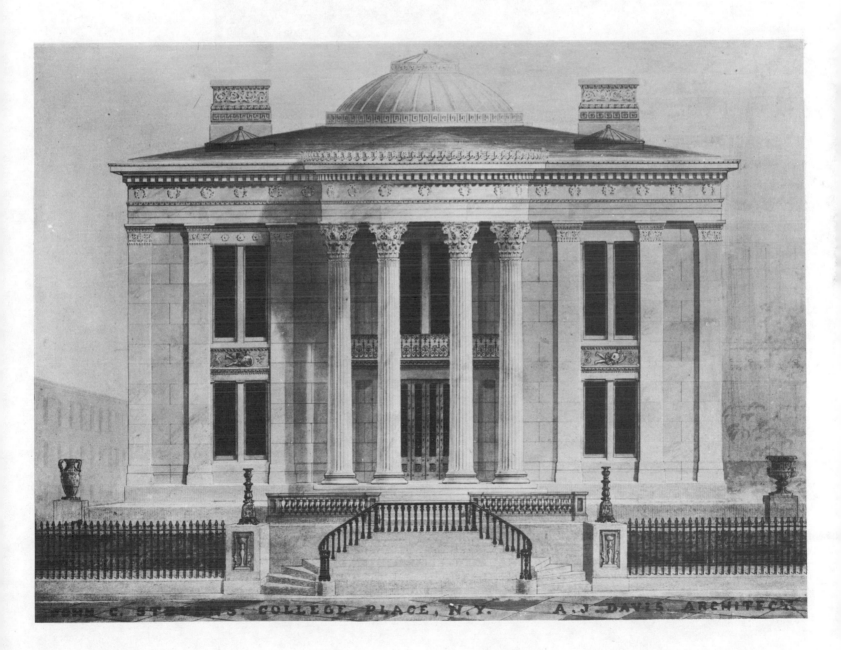

1

PRIME HOUSE.   With wood the commonest construction material for country estates, large houses often took their form as much from the logic of building in timber as from the modes of Gothic or Greek Revival. The old Prime house was built in 1800, overlooking the East River at the foot of 89th Street. The pictures show opposite sides, probably the driveway frontage (1) and the eastern river frontage (2).

2

BREVOORT HOUSE. One of the best-known mansion houses was this one for Henry Brevoort at the northwest corner of 9th Street and Fifth Avenue, built in 1834 and probably designed by the firm of Ithiel Town and A. J. Davis. Although it was freestanding — in fact there was a garden entrance on one side and a curved window bay on the other — its crisp design could have made it a model for later New York row houses. But the building's plainness was not simplicity. Its Greek key cornice ornament and the paneled front wall were original ideas. In 1925, with the name temporarily assured of survival in the Brevoort Hotel (see page 42), the Brevoort house was torn down to make way for another hotel.

HALF AND HALF HOUSE.   Before iron was widely used in construction, the difference between a wood and a masonry house was quite small. In both cases, except in the unlikely event that masonry vaulting supported the floors, all the internal spans and usually all interior walls were of timber. Only the exterior walls might be masonry. The difference in construction between the brick and the clapboard halves of the Colonel Kopper house, which stood on 124th Street between Third and Lexington Avenues, was really only skin deep — but it would be hard to imagine a blunter demonstration of the use of expensive materials for the front part of a building only. The house dated from 1790, and was by Johann Hermann Raub.

WHEELOCK HOUSE. Eclecticism, a philosophical concept originating in France in the 1830s, described a system of thought composed of elements selected from other systems. The idea was internationally adapted to architecture, in the belief that a rational selection of historical forms could be assembled to create a whole building which would then be appropriate for modern use. The house built about 1860 by William A. Wheelock in New York at 661 West 158th Street was an enthusiastic example of the Eclectic mode — the ogee roofs, inventive ornament, circular and flattened window heads were all vital characteristics. It survived on Riverside Drive only through the late 1930s.

FIFTH AVENUE, NORTH FROM 65TH STREET.   By 1898, Fifth Avenue from 46th Street to 72nd Street was an almost uninterrupted mile and a half of palazzi, chateaux and fortresses, bordering Central Park. Richard Morris Hunt's house for Mrs. John Jacob Astor and William B. Astor is at the right in the photograph, and beyond that lived Haights, Goulds, Millses, Belmonts, on and on to the north — a visual summary of free enterprise and the history of architecture. This staggering parade of wealth has been drastically altered by the replacement of most of the buildings by tall apartment houses.

1

VANDERBILT HOUSES.   By 1880, the Vanderbilt fortune was the greatest ever amassed in America. William Henry Vanderbilt, son of the Commodore, had two great houses built for him by Gustav and Christian Herter on Fifth Avenue from 51st to 52nd Streets (1, left). The twin houses, built in 1880–84, were divided by an atrium that separated the W. H. Vanderbilt residence from that of his two sons-in-law, Elliott F. Shepard and William D. Sloane. Across 52nd Street to the north was Richard Morris Hunt's house for William Kissam Vanderbilt (1, right), William Henry's son, built 1879–81. Concurrently, Cornelius Vanderbilt II (also son of William Henry) had the first part of George B. Post's

2

design under way for himself on 57th Street (see pages 24 and 111). It was said that $15,000,000 was expended on the building, decoration and furnishing of the Vanderbilt houses.

One of the specific objectives of the Vanderbilts was to build a more staggering house than A. T. Stewart had done (facing page). Considering their outlay, this was relatively easy. William Henry Vanderbilt had included in his house an art gallery (2) to which the public was admitted by card on Thursdays. The visual feast guests were able to enjoy within the gallery included exotic marbles, mother-of-pearl, glass, gold and polychrome — the room, according to a contemporary publication, was "an important element in cultivating the artistic taste of the metropolis."

The William K. Vanderbilt house was demolished in 1925, and the last half of the Vanderbilt twins vanished in 1947.

THE A. T. STEWART HOUSE.   Alexander Turney Stewart, celebrated as a tightwad and grouch, nevertheless contributed three notable buildings to New York: his hotel for working women which became the Park Avenue Hotel (see page 66), his department store (page 168), and his home, on the northwest corner of 34th Street and Fifth Avenue. The Stewart mansion, built in 1864–69 by John W. Kellum, architect of all three, was the least comely of the buildings — $3,000,000 of marble and Civil War-period pomp. The Grand Hall heading toward his art gallery was filled with unmistakably parvenu art. After the death of Stewart's widow the building was torn down in 1901 to make room for the old Knickerbocker Trust Company's bank.

MARY MASON JONES HOUSE. Between 57th and 58th Streets on the east side of Fifth Avenue was "Marble Row" (see page 26), a rich man's housing project planned by Mary Mason Jones, whose banker father had paid the city $1500 for the site in 1825. The white marble houses were built by the architect Robert Mook in 1867–69. Mrs. Jones herself occupied the corner house at 57th Street shown in this photograph. The house, the owner, and Mrs. Paran Stevens, the next occupant, all figured in Edith Wharton's fiction in slight disguise. By the '90s the commercial possibilities of the row had become irresistible, and the corner pavilion at 58th Street was made into a bank. The handsome row vanished altogether in 1929.

THE SENATOR CLARK HOUSE.　　One of the more ephemeral of New York's expendable buildings was the solid-looking William A. Clark house on the northeast corner of Fifth Avenue and 77th Street. Senator Clark of Montana, a copper king, hired the sophisticated architects Lord, Hewlett & Hull and K. M. Murchison to come to terms with his desires, a proposition that took six years and ultimately also involved H. Deglane of Paris. The result of their labors was completed in 1904: a building faced mostly in white granite and said to contain 130 rooms. The house immediately fell under attack in gossip and print, twice in *Collier's* alone the following year, which printed satirical poems about its alleged vulgarity. Only twenty-three years after it had been built, the structure vanished, and Senator Clark's collection of decorative treasures left ungrateful New York for Washington. Most, including the house's sumptuous early 18th-century Salon Doré, can now be seen at the Corcoran Gallery of Art.

THE SCHWAB HOUSE. Compared to Fifth Avenue, the allurement of Riverside Drive took longer to bloom and faded more quickly. Its charms included proximity to Morningside Heights ("the Acropolis of America" in the '90s), and a great west-facing view of the sunset behind the Hudson Palisades. Frederick Law Olmsted had sponsored the design for Riverside Park on land acquired by the city after 1872, and though at the turn of the century trees were still low and the Drive itself seemingly far too wide, many wealthy men had already responded to the attractiveness of the upper West Side.

This was the situation to which Charles M. Schwab committed himself when he built his enormous Riverside Drive mansion in 1902–06, with Maurice Hebert as architect. The property was the entire block north of 73rd Street. But the far West Side was borderland — a strip of valuable fortified houses with lines of communication only back to downtown; cut off even from nearby Central Park West, another affluent border. Between the two park edges multiple dwellings became overcrowded and run down, and Riverside Drive lost its chance of surpassing Fifth Avenue's demonstration of wealth. The Schwab house was empty in 1947 and has been replaced by an apartment house.

THE BROKAW MANSIONS.   The greatest cry for preservation in New York arose in September, 1964, when the Brokaw mansions, houses at 984 Fifth Avenue, 1 East 79th Street, and 7 East 79th Street, were announced for demolition; and again in February, 1965, when the work of razing was begun on a weekend. The disposition of the old Brokaw property became an issue prominently discussed in New York newspapers and a number of magazines. The outcry was undoubtedly what at last induced the mayor to sign the law giving the Landmarks Commission legal powers, and that fact is the most distinguished landmark quality the Brokaw mansions ever had.

Isaac Vail Brokaw, a clothing manufacturer and real estate man, had the corner house built according to plans by Rose & Stone in 1887–88 (with roof off in the picture). He subsequently ordered two adjacent

houses to the north (1905, by Charles F. Rose) for two sons, and an adjacent house to the east for a daughter (1911), the architect H. Van Buren Magonigle. The northernmost house at 985 Fifth Avenue is still standing.

Apart from their considerable interior amenities, the only house of the group with a degree of real merit was Brokaw's first. There was dignity and rugged solidity in the old castle, though it was not nearly as skillful a design as Hunt's Vanderbilt chateau on 52nd Street (see page 121). The most important thing about the Brokaw mansions on the urban scene was the way they marked a very important corner. At the crossroads of Fifth Avenue and the 79th Street-Central Park Transverse, they made a reassuringly rich pile of masonry where one turned from East 79th Street up to the Metropolitan Museum.

127

THE NEW YORK ROW HOUSE.

As the gridiron of streets and the subway system extended, houses were built from block to block. The type of house favored by the speculative builders was attached to its neighbors. This row-house type allowed for great economies in land use, since many could be built side by side on narrow street frontage. The typical New York block dimension of 200 by 600 to 800 feet also permitted relatively deep buildings, each with a rear yard, on all four sides of the block. The corners suited larger developments.

The one-family row house was also very economical to build. Common walls which separated the houses carried the floor loads, and the walls were no further apart than necessary for cheap timber floor joist spans. Almost the only surfaces which could be called architectural problems were the front and rear walls. The rear wall was inevitably brick, but after the 1860s the finish material on the front was sometimes limestone and often brownstone, a type of sandstone usually obtained from a now played-out vein in New Jersey. While soft and easily eroded, brownstone could be patched and repaired with colored cement. Compared with the frequent treatment of terrace houses in London and Bath, there were few historic attempts in New York to visually combine ranges of row houses. The idea that many houses should be treated to look like one wide palace must have been taken as more appropriate for the side of a square than for a linear street. What could be called comprehensive design in New York merely amounted to the rough alignment of adjacent cornice heights and masonry stringcourses, while the limitations of height imposed by wall bearing and stair climbing also served to unify designs.

As one-family town houses, the New York row house seemed ideal. Wealthier families could have carriages and stables, but the liveability of the basic type was within reach of many. The row houses that remain are highly valued today, and are likely to increase further in value — both to the owners and to the city — as other resident types become ever more predominant.

Some typical speculative row houses near Lenox Avenue on West 133rd Street, about 1882. These were built for single-family occupancy according to a conventional plan. Within fifteen years most of the vacant sites had been filled with similar houses. Buildings of this type are rapidly vanishing all over the city.

LA GRANGE TERRACE (*"COLONNADE ROW"*).   Lafayette Street was once Lafayette Place, a short, wide residential enclave, and only later city developments cut it into the commercial conduit that it is today. In 1830 it was comely enough to be a likely site for speculative development, and Seth Geer hired an architect to design nine houses for him there, running up to 47 Lafayette Place (now 434 Lafayette Street) and completed in 1833. The Terrace has often been attributed to A. J. Davis, but recent evidence suggests that it may have been the work of Robert Higham, an Albany architect associated with Philip Hooker.

Whoever the designer, there is persuasive reason to believe that he conceived of the twenty-eight free-standing Corinthian columns as an architectural ensemble. Like the columniated buildings of Playfair in Edinburgh, the Woods in Bath, or Smirke in London, La Grange Terrace (named after Lafayette's country home) was a unified work — as great as any of theirs for the simplicity of the architect's subject and the grandeur he gave it. The destruction of five-ninths of the Terrace in 1901 to make way for Wanamaker's warehouse can therefore be taken as the destruction of his intent. The rump four houses are now designated as Landmarks.

UNDERHILL'S COLONNADE BUILDINGS.   In 1837 Brooklyn was another city, and in that period, long before the Brooklyn Bridge was built, New York was already an admirable sight from its high coast. The row of Greek Revival houses built around that time on Brooklyn's Columbia Heights near Middagh Street was perhaps influenced by La Grange Terrace, but the unifying beauty of its colonnade was here less of benefit to its occupants than it was a gift to the New Yorkers across the East River.

This picture was used as an advertisement for the houses, though the unexplained fire indicates its original purpose may have been different. Underhill's Colonnade, long gone, appeared in many views of the river scene.

HOUSES WITH PITCHED ROOFS. "A great number of excellent private dwellings are built of red painted brick, which gives them a peculiarly neat and clean appearance," a London visitor to New York wrote in 1819. The characteristic house was two or three stories high, sometimes twenty-five feet wide, two rooms deep, with a pitched roof and delicate dormers. These, built long before the Civil War, were at 512–514 Broome Street, and are now gone.

HOUSES WITH WOODEN PORCHES. From the middle of the 19th century, roofs were sometimes metal, frequently flat or slightly pitched, and hidden behind a raised cornice. The row house got to be a higher building than it had generally been before. The gridiron street layout of the 1811 Commissioners' Plan was an accomplished fact. One effect of the gridiron was to insure that most house plots would be a uniform 100 feet deep. Another was that few houses would possess a vista. New York row houses consequently adapted themselves to site conditions by taking great account of available open space, both in developing the rear garden, and — sometimes — by increasing the privacy of the front. A way of doing this was by building on exterior porches, which also gave the standard double-room depth an extra space and dimension. Many Greenwich Village brick row houses had wooden porches, usually in the rear. The vanished "Cottage Row" shown, on Seventh Avenue between 12th and 13th Streets, had them in front (the row was built about 1850, and had ornamental railings which were removed in 1931). The houses were designed in a unit, as indicated by the dentil blocks uniformly under the cornice and the symmetrical projection of the center and end bays.

LONDON TERRACE.   The London Terrace houses, on the north side of 23rd Street between Ninth and Tenth Avenues, were designed for William Torrey in 1845 by A. J. Davis. They were uniformly pilastered to give the effect of a colonnade from one avenue to the other, and were set back about thirty-five feet from the street, with gardens in front. Similar buildings, known as "Chelsea Cottages," were on the 24th Street side of the block. This property was all eradicated by the block of flats that now bears the London Terrace name.

RHINELANDER GARDENS.   This row of houses was at 110–124 West 11th Street, between Sixth and Seventh Avenues. It was built in 1854 by James Renwick, architect also of Grace Church and St. Patrick's. Its tiers of cast-iron balconies unified the street facade much as did the columns of La Grange Terrace, or the wall pillars of London Terrace. In a way Rhinelander Gardens was even more prepossessing than those others, because its ironwork was the beautiful product of a machine technology, later called more and more into architectural use. The setback fronts of the houses were the result of the imperfect match of the old Greenwich Village street pattern with the upper Manhattan grid. Some deep fronts can still be seen on 11th Street, but the Rhinelander row was demolished in the late 1950s.

MANSARDED TERRACE. The block of speculative row houses on Fifth Avenue between 55th and 56th Streets was a bit less grand, but otherwise similar in many ways to the mansions of "Marble Row" (see page 26); it was finished in the same year (1869), had mansard roofs, and was also clad in marble. This terrace was one story higher and was the work of a distinguished architect, the Danish-American Detlef Lienau. In addition to his use of the currently fancied roof shape, Lienau designed the various levels as superimposed architectural orders.

THE BROWNSTONES. In *Things As They Are in America*, William Chambers, the Edinburgh publisher of *Chambers's Encyclopaedia*, said this about New York in 1853: "Wherever any of [the] older brick edifices have been removed, their place has been supplied by tenements [dwellings] built of brown sandstone; and it may be said that at present New York is in process of being renewed by this species of structure . . ." The older brick buildings were usually painted red with white joints (which was really more durable, since brownstone spalled in freezing weather). But the choice of brownstone for cladding the Vanderbilt twins (see page 121) finally confirmed the material's stylish supremacy. By the 1880s, New York had become a red and brown city as Bath was cream and London black and white. With the main brownstone quarries now no longer open, "brownstones" — the remaining terrace houses faced with the material — are quickly vanishing without an echo.

APARTMENT HOUSES.

Frank Lloyd Wright's Broadacre City project envisioned a place where everyone would have his separate house and plot. His design was a reaction to modern cities, where most people must live in multiple dwellings. High population densities, and hence apartment house developments, were inevitable under conditions where land values were increasing, transportation was poor, and rental accommodations were acceptable — the loss of a back yard and a personal front door to the street could be measured against the big advantages of apartment life, with its potential social vitality and convenient urban location. New York produced two noteworthy early models of apartment houses. One was a sort of communal palace, typified by the Dakota (which still stands, on Central Park West and 72nd Street). This building type had every comfort of a private great house but was developed in multiple form, and with the services of a grand hotel added. Extraordinary measures were taken to insure the privacy and isolation of separate suites, to make community life not too trying.

The other New York paradigm was the Old-Law tenement. In a sense this was also built as an accurate response to the requirements of life. Early "railroad flats" with only the end rooms receiving light and air succumbed to the Tenement House Law of 1879, the barely restrictive "old law." The demand for cheap housing led to the development of a special building form to suit the law, which exploited land and the adaptability of its inhabitants to the fullest. Since real estate was sold on the basis of street frontage, very deep narrow buildings were the most profitable. With the stair in the center, a long strip of rooms could be run from front to back on each side. These rooms became either two or four apartments per floor, with public toilets on the landing. The stairway and the shafts to let air and a little light down to the inside rooms gave the apartments a characteristic dumbbell-plan shape. Within the apartments one room opened directly into another. Front doors were often set at an angle to keep the public passageway at the minimum possible width.

These early multiple dwellings became characteristic New York types. When a refined apartment house design at last began to appear, a sort of compromise between the rich and poor extremes, the buildings were called French Flats, because there was no American precedent. The acceptance of French Flats by the public was historically significant. Their eventual profusion established middle-class urban society at a new density in American cities. The New York communal palaces and Old-Law tenements are now rapidly disappearing, elegant brontosauruses and grim pterodactyls among the more highly refined evolutionary building forms.

The Navarro Flats, Central Park South and Seventh Avenue, designed by Hubert, Pirsson & Co., built in 1882. To help reduce the fashionable prejudice toward apartment life, it was built and operated as a group of individual houses, known as the Madrid, Granada, Lisbon, Cordova, Barcelona, Valencia, Salamanca and Tolosa. It was destroyed to provide a site for a new building.

THE "OLD-LAW TENEMENTS." New York is well rid of some of its vanishing buildings. When the new 1901 Tenement House Law was passed, there were about 86,000 buildings in the city which the new law declared substandard. They were mostly supreme exploitation properties. Under the old law, it was possible to build a house for $25,000 on a 25 by 100 foot lot that housed a dozen families, or two dozen in some neighborhoods. Moses King's 1893 *Handbook of New York City*, noting the wide distribution of tenements, pointed out that "In a single block between Avenue B and Avenue C and 2nd and 3rd Streets there are over 3,500 residents, and a smaller block on Houston Street contains 3,000 people, which is at the rate of 1,000,000 to the square mile." This density was achieved in buildings usually no more than six stories high, which makes the packing of people even more incredible than it would seem today. In 1891 the Board of Health found that two-thirds of the entire population of the city were living in tenements, according to King's *Handbook*. Some tenements were better than others (and "the city" before 1898 was not Greater New York), but it is clear that misery and overcrowding was the condition of the majority. Although the new law made such slum houses forbidden, the law was not retroactively effective on this better-lost aspect of New York. Immigration and other population pressures — as well as continued profitability — keep about half of the Old-Law tenements still intact today, such as most of those on Henry Street (1) and 100th Street (2).

1

STUDIO BUILDING.   There are various claims as to which building in New York was the first multiple dwelling, but undoubtedly the first building specialized to provide artists' studios — living quarters were included — was the Studio Building, at 51–55 West 10th Street, designed by Richard Morris Hunt (who was later responsible for the W. K. Vanderbilt house — page 121). Hunt was headmost in the procession of American architects to study at the École des Beaux-Arts, and he had returned from Paris just two years prior to construction of the Studio in 1857. His client was James Boorman Johnson, and the building became a virtual clubhouse of the Hudson River School. Its popularity was evident when it later became a cooperative, and the building's importance was the first demonstration that high, well-lit rooms would be welcome in New York apartments. After having housed John LaFarge, Frederick Church, and Winslow Homer (among scores of others), the Studio was demolished in 1954.

THE KNICKERBOCKER.   The Knickerbocker, now vanished, is said to have been one of New York's first cooperative apartment houses. It was on Fifth Avenue at 28th Street, built there when the Madison Square area was still fashionable. Ernest Flagg, architect of the building, was also the accomplished designer of the still extant little Singer building at 88 Prince Street, the former Scribner's (now Benneton) at 597 Fifth Avenue, and the lost Singer Tower (see pages 212–13).

CHURCHES.

In recent years, as the pattern of urban settlement changed and quantities of New Yorkers moved off to the suburbs, church and synagogue leaders could be heard explaining church relocation moves by pointing out to the public that a religious establishment was not a *building* at all really, it was a *congregation*. This was fair warning that a church was soon to be sold. Though religious institutions are not taxed, central urban property represents a considerable frozen asset to a congregation seeking to establish itself elsewhere. Without the state interest in religion that operates in cities such as London and Rome, churches in New York have been subjected to the same economic imperatives and forces as corporations. Sanctified ground seems less sanctified when the real estate value soars. This problem has been a source of worry to St. Paul's Chapel on Broadway and Fulton Street, and to the once-endangered Friends Meeting House on East 20th Street at Gramercy Park.

New York has had a quite remarkable number of fine churches and synagogues destroyed. Some of the most stylish period buildings in America — the Greek and Gothic Revival churches on this and the facing page, for example, and such authentic masterpieces as St. John's — have been sold and demolished. It would probably be beyond the scope of urban conservation policy to arrange for the continuous use of churches that are no longer serving a local population, but a preservation program that is supported by church groups would be a welcome change in attitude. Churches were deeply significant buildings in the early formation of New York, and are still essential elements of the public patrimony.

The Jones Chapel (1), on East 64th Street, was built about 1830. The Mount Washington Church (2), at Broadway and Dyckman Street, was built in 1844 and enlarged in 1856. Each building was an elegantly characteristic example, in timber, of a revival mode. Both are now gone.

1

2

THE OLD BRICK CHURCH.   The Brick Presbyterian Church by John McComb, Sr. was on the northeast corner of Beekman and Nassau Streets. Its picture here, from *Frank Leslie's Illustrated* in 1856, was engraved on the occasion of rumors of its imminent destruction to make way for a post office. The land then was "probably the most valuable in the city." The post office deal apparently fell through, but the congregation managed to sell the property to the *New York Times* which put up a building on the site in 1857–58. The old Brick Church had been there since 1767.

THE MIDDLE DUTCH CHURCH.　　Revival modes were at their most spectacular in New York's religious buildings.　The old Elm Street Synagogue, for example, was a three-bay Doric temple, on top of which was a perfect little English Perpendicular cupola.　The Middle Dutch Church, however — finished in 1839 on Lafayette Place, near La Grange Terrace — was a single-mindedly classic Greek Revival church by Isaiah Rogers, perhaps his best work (see also page 68).　Unfortunately for posterity, the Dutch Reformed (Collegiate) denomination was wealthy enough to move as frequently as the neighborhood ran down.　This church's forerunner was built in 1729 at Nassau Street, later became the Post Office, and was demolished in 1882.　After the Lafayette Place church was evacuated in 1887 prior to its destruction, a third church was erected at Second Avenue and 7th Street, "thoroughly equipped," as one guide said, "with reading-rooms, gymnasium, and all appliances for aggressive modern church work."

1

MADISON SQUARE PRESBYTERIAN CHURCH. McKim, Mead and White designed a new Byzantine Madison Square Presbyterian Church (1) to take the place of the old Gothic one at the southeast corner of Madison Avenue and 24th Street, which was in the way of the Metropolitan Life Tower. The new church was completed in 1906 at the northeast corner of Madison Avenue and 24th Street (2); but in a few years that, too, was gone.

2

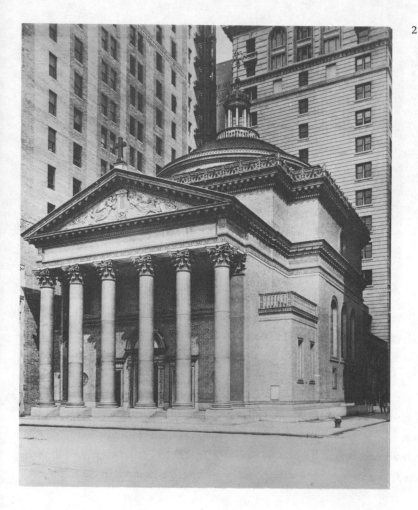

DR. TYNG'S CHURCH.   The Episcopal Church of the Holy Trinity was built by a parish founded in 1864 by the younger Stephen H. Tyng, a hardworking New York churchman. The congregation hired the Prague-born Leopold Eidlitz as architect, an exponent of a sort of Germanic Romanesque design. Dr. Tyng's Church, as the now demolished building was usually called, was completed in 1874 on the northeast corner of Madison Avenue and 42nd Street — just a block from the first Grand Central Station, which is seen in the distance (and on page 28).

TEMPLE EMANU-EL, 43RD STREET. This photograph, one of fifty-seven wide angle pictures of as many blocks on Fifth Avenue, was taken by the Byron Company in 1924 but not rediscovered until 1962. The series was commissioned by a real estate firm to commemorate the 100th anniversary of Fifth Avenue, the first section of which was completed in 1824. The building on the right, at the northeast corner of 43rd Street, is Temple Emanu-El, long considered one of the finest synagogues in the world. By Leopold Eidlitz in association with Henry Fernbach, the building was erected in 1866–68. The temple was "Moorish," with Saracenic arches over columns inside, spanning a space for a congregation of nearly 2,000. But the land was enormously valuable. A year after this picture was made the congregation was looking for another home. The Eidlitz-Fernbach building was demolished in 1927, and a new temple, on 65th Street and Fifth Avenue, was dedicated in 1930.

150

ST. JOHN'S CHAPEL. St. John's (1), a church worthy of rank with St. Paul's, was built by the vestrymen of Trinity parish in 1803. It was the masterpiece of John McComb, Jr., who later improved Castle Clinton (page 96) and collaborated on the New York City Hall. Here his collaborator

1

was his brother Isaac. The interior of the church was as fine as the Georgian St. Paul's, which in fact St. John's much resembled (2). The chancel was built in 1857 by Richard M. Upjohn. The chapel spire, of hewn oak and with a town clock, rose above the surrounding buildings, 214½ feet high. A Corinthian portico with four large columns of sandstone stood in front.

In the first years of the church a park was laid out before it, bounded by Varick, Beach, Hudson and Laight Streets and called Hudson Square, or St. John's Park. It was improved and fenced by the property owners who had built substantial houses around it. The photograph of St. John's Park (3), made about the time of the Civil War, shows it shortly before it was sold by the city to Commodore Vanderbilt. In 1867 he covered the entire site with four acres of train sidings and the Hudson River Railroad Freight Depot (4). Virtually none of the neighborhood residents remained. A writer in the '90s found St. John's Chapel the only church within a great area, surrounded by factories and tenements. The church and a few houses adjacent remained standing until 1918, when the city carelessly destroyed them while widening Varick Street.

3
4

MOVEMENT.

The vitality of cities depends first of all on the richness of their communications networks, for it is through these that encounters are made to permit shopping, recreation, working, and every other urban activity. Before the telephone revolutionized communications, it was necessary to travel to communicate instantly, and some kind of movement between people and goods still accounts for most urban contacts. It follows that many different kinds of transportation should be encouraged in order to facilitate as many opportunities as possible for diverse communication. Not only is this a requirement to make a place dynamic and interesting, but it also provides for much smoother operations in the daily life of the city, eliminating bottlenecks by providing intentional plurality and overlapping of function. A man on West 59th Street knows he can get to the theater on West 45th Street within twenty minutes, because he can either walk, or take a taxi, subway, bus, or he can get there in a combination of ways. If only one of these alternatives were available, he would probably need to allow himself much more time because of congestion or the possibility of unforeseen delay.

While some means of transportation (such as the horse and cart) have obviously become obsolete, others are permitted to wither when they could and should be actively sustained. Pedestrian walks have been systematically eliminated whenever they have vied for space with motor traffic. The Triborough Bridge and Tunnel Authority decided that the new Verrazano–Narrows Bridge did not need a pedestrian walk; one can therefore never stop on the bridge to see a stunning view of the harbor. The same agency widened the roadway on theWhitestone Bridge and eliminated the walk shown in the photograph on the opposite page. The Port of New York Authority left the originally planned rapid transit line off the second deck of the George Washington Bridge.

Communications possibilities not only ought to be obtainable, but should be *seen* to be obtainable. There should be no secret about the route taken by a bus, the identification of a taxi (New York is very good about this), the location of a railroad station or subway stop or phone booth. Great communications centers and movement terminals require explicit architecture. The city's clarity and operation are disabled when the forms and patterns of diverse movement are destroyed.

The Bronx-Whitestone Bridge spans the East River, linking the Bronx with Queens. It was built in 1937–39, by Othmar H. Ammann and Allston Dana, engineers, and Aymar Embury II, architect, with provision for pedestrian and vehicular traffic. Precautionary wind bracing was subsequently added to the edges of the deck, thus obstructing the view off the bridge, and sidewalks were eliminated to provide three motor lanes in each direction.

TRAIN SHED.   The British first put railroads to use. Most of the great British railroad stations were built in the 1850s and '60s, and while none of them was as notably palatial as New York's later Pennsylvania Station, they in fact usually followed a different plan principle. The ticket office and waiting rooms were in a masonry front. Connected, but often entirely unrelated to it architecturally (and sometimes not even designed by architects), was the train shed. This was a great canopy of iron and glass; at its best — as in York and Paddington — taking the form of vaults that curved not only in section but in plan, so the effect was like walking within a coiled spring.

The 1871 Grand Central train shed, shown here, was inspired by such stations. John B. Snook was the architect, Isaac C. Buckhout the engineer. The cast and wrought iron arches, spanning 200 feet, were far loftier than those of most great stations in Britain. Though the train shed inevitably had to be removed in 1906 to make way for functional changes (see pages 28 and 31), the clarity of its great cylindrical form was never surpassed in later building.

DOUBLE-DECKER BUS. Ease of access to public transportation — now being recommended for cities in the form of monorails, electric taxis and minibuses — was available in New York when public transportation was the only kind that most people could get. From about 1890 to 1920, open-sided trolleys were widely used which could be boarded from anywhere along their sides whenever they went slowly. The trolleys' need for a non-driving conductor made their manpower requirements high, and the last vanished from the Central Park West line in the '30s.

The double-decker bus was a public vehicle which abided longer. In its motorized form it was run by the Fifth Avenue Coach Company from 1907 until 1946. The double-deckers allowed a sensible saving of space on the crowded avenue, and the ones with open tops were magnificent in all kinds of weather. Like the open-sided trolleys, the old double-deckers also had a conductor for fares, but if they were boarded between stops, at least it was more likely to be from the sidewalk. According to the Fifth Avenue Association's book *Fifty Years on Fifth*, they were abandoned for the very reason they should be reinstituted: "Because of the interminable rides taken by the bewitched."

HUDSON FERRIES.   Before the Holland Tunnel was built, there were thirty-eight Manhattan ferry lines, besides upstream and freight lines. Ferries were the only means of communication between Manhattan and the west. The first Hoboken ferry was established in 1774, and after the introduction of steam ferryboats to New York in 1814, that Hudson crossing became the major one. Access to New Jersey was available at eleven ferry points below 24th Street. The number of crossing points was a great convenience for passengers, a transit versatility unmatched by the motor vehicle routes that put the ferries out of business. This photograph shows the Hoboken ferry terminal, run by the Erie–Lackawanna Railroad, at the foot of 23rd Street.

SUBWAY ENTRANCES.   Subways have proved the most practical, most serviceable —
and most nerve-deadening — way of moving around New York. Since the (now abandoned) elegant
City Hall station of the IRT was built in 1904, it seems that no further attempt was ever made to build
a system for use by people. Apart from the plainness of the stations and passageways, the complex networks, frequent stairs, dead-end alcoves, lack of passenger direction planning, variety of structural devices,
poor choices of materials, noise of equipment, and lack of signs make the New York subway perhaps the
worst piece of public design work in the civilized world — one obvious reason why it is often vandal-
ridden and dangerous as well.

Postscript 2000: My 1967 comments above might be slightly softened in view of some recent improvements. Nevertheless, one of the few humanely designed parts of the old system, the iron and glass
subway kiosks that protected descending passengers from wind and emerging ones from rain, were all
removed in the late 1960s. Designed by Heins & LaFarge in 1904, the entranceways (as shown) had
curved cast-iron roofs; the exitway kiosks had pyramidal glass roofs.

COMMERCE.

Commercial buildings provide the best case for urban conservation, as distinguished from preservation. Since they have no important function other than efficient operation for profit, it would be very expensive, even if practical, for anyone to subsidize *preservation* in commerce once operations had become uneconomical. Yet if key commercial buildings and districts were treated as long-term *conservation* problems, normal government powers (such as taxation, zoning, development of communications improvements) could be used to aid their continuing efficient use.

Many lost commercial buildings in New York have been destroyed because management needed more space or better communications and consequently moved out, with the result that specialized and elegant buildings left behind found no willing users. The New York Herald building was one such example (see page 169). Such losses could be kept to a minimum with an active municipal commercial development program that had conservation of urban form as one of its avowed aims.

Another frequent cause of unnecessary demolition occurs primarily in rental rather than self-tenanted properties. Buildings are torn down to be replaced by new buildings of greater floor area, or by another building type that currently provides higher returns. This happened to the old German Savings Bank building (see page 165). If it is actually against the general public welfare for such changes to take place, existing use and bulk ought to be defended with zoning laws. These laws are now on the books, but permissive interpretations in the past have rarely limited a developer's goals. Better than compulsory government powers would be tax advantages, rigged to encourage building on underdeveloped sites rather than rebuilding on well developed ones. This would not only create a broader base for taxation; the appearance and good use of efficient business districts could be also thereby maintained.

Older commercial buildings are frequently simpler to alter than technically sophisticated new ones. A conservation attitude would encourage the maintenance of old buildings and keep them fit for continuing use. Rather than limit new construction, this would lead to more healthy growth and change.

Pier of the French Line. This interior — showing pointed arch timber truss construction — was probably at the pier of the Compagnie Générale Transatlantique when it was located on West Street between Horatio and Jane Streets. The French Line piers are now uptown, and this early structure has been replaced by a steel-framed pier.

WESTERN UNION.   The now vanished Western Union building was built in 1873–75 at Broadway and Dey Street, George B. Post the architect. The Western Union and the New York Tribune buildings have been called the first skyscrapers, since both were the earliest ordinary commercial structures to incorporate elevators. The ten-story, 230-foot Western Union building was also one of the first buildings to face the stylistic problem of what to do with all that slenderness. For the time being, the solution seemed to be to make the top third a rather splendid Renaissance palace.

Overhead wire networks grew thicker and thicker until the late '80s, when most were put underground in conduits.

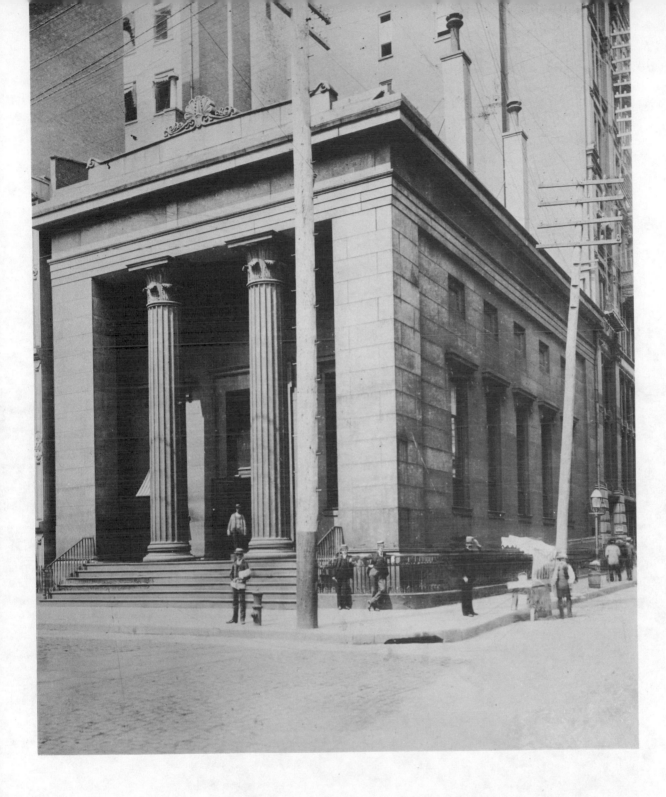

BANK OF AMERICA.   The innovation of the elevator (and later the steel skeleton) caused many property owners to look less fondly at their properties, particularly if they were on very valuable downtown sites. Many landmarks of commerce were scrapped in favor of added floor space. One such was the building shown above, the 1835 Bank of America at the northwest corner of Wall and William Streets. In 1889 it was replaced by a nine-story successor that not only provided more room for the bank, but had offices to rent. In the new elevator buildings every floor was equally accessible, a revolutionary development in real estate as well as architecture, since rental possibilities suddenly reached up beyond the lowest two levels.

WORTH STREET. The block of Worth Street between Broadway and Church Street once contained a row of cast-iron front commercial buildings, the finest such group east of St. Louis. Most were built around 1869 by the architect Griffith Thomas as dry-goods warehouses, but they soon became the New York textile center. When the garment district developed uptown the immense wholesale activity of the block was stilled, with only a few fabric houses remaining there. Most of the block was razed in 1963 for a parking lot.

THE GERMAN SAVINGS BANK.   The thin elements, sharp detail, and high relief possible with the use of cast-iron elements made for a new kind of light but vigorous architectural expression that affected even conventional construction, and large glass areas were attempted as well in masonry buildings such as the German Savings Bank, at the southeast corner of 14th Street and Fourth Avenue. It was built in 1870–72, with Henry Fernbach the architect. An apartment house now occupies the site.

ECCENTRIC MILL WORKS.   James Bogardus (1800–1874), watchmaker, inventor
builder of towers (see page 93), "Architect in Iron" as he called himself in his 1858 booklet *Cast-Iron
Buildings — Their Construction and Advantages*, keeps New York from second place to either Chicago or
London in the invention and development of iron in building. He devised and popularized a prefabricated
system of cast-iron elements for factory buildings which are the ancestors of Lever and Seagram.
Bogardus was a system-builder who saw no limit to the use of cast iron. The last of his New York
buildings has now vanished (see page 202). This print shows the eccentric grinding-mill manufactory
he built for his own use, which had a complete metal frame, including prefabricated piers, columns,
beams and wall panels. It was completed in 1849 at the corner of Centre and Duane Streets in only
weeks of assembly time, and was disassembled again ten years later when Duane Street was widened —
a now-vanished landmark of modern architecture. Bogardus's later conception of an advanced structure for the 1853 New York World's Fair involving a circular catenary chain-supported roof was
rejected in favor of the imitative Crystal Palace (see pages 182–83).

HARPER'S, FRANKLIN SQUARE.   Bogardus's most elaborate commission was executed in 1854 for the Harper & Brothers building at 331 Pearl Street in Franklin Square, which was razed in 1920. A fire had completely destroyed the publisher's plant in 1853, and even though the fatal weakness of iron construction in a fire was not then well understood, Bogardus and John B. Corlies, the collaborating architect, did a thorough job of reducing danger on the new building.

It was not a complete iron fabrication system as the Eccentric Mill Works had been, since it used masonry in the facade and in load bearing. But Bogardus continued to demonstrate his inventive imagination in the girders he designed for Harper's. Cast iron, while strong in compression, is crystalline and consequently very brittle. If long cast-iron beams or girders had any flaw in them, they cracked open from the bottom. The girders Bogardus provided were of cast iron shaped like arches, with rods along the bottom of wrought iron, a far more elastic material. Soon wrought-iron rolling mills were turning out full-sized structural members, but Bogardus's inventiveness foreshadowed the use of extra-strength steels in parts of modern buildings.

THE A. T. STEWART STORE.   John W. Kellum was one of the many architects who worked in cast iron in the '50s. His 1859 department store for A. T. Stewart east of Broadway between 9th and 10th Streets (later half of Wanamaker's, and the scene of a spectacular fire during demolition in 1956) was a complete iron frame structure manufactured by the Cornell Iron Works, one of the most extensive buildings ever done in that material, and one of the simplest in appearance.

1

2

THE NEW YORK HERALD BUILDING. McKim, Mead and White designed this Venetian palazzo for James Gordon Bennett. It was erected at Broadway and 35th Street (Herald Square) in 1893. The delicate building was stuffed with printing presses which could be admired from the arcades. Its famous clock is the only part of the public-spirited design that survives — now at the south end of the square.

1

2

THE TIMES TOWER.   The Times Tower (1) was begun in 1903 in what was then Longacre Square. Completed in 1905, it was twenty-five stories high, and New York's second tallest structure. It was also known as "the second Flatiron building," because of its shape — both buildings being characteristic of Broadway's acute-angle intersection with avenues. The *New York Times* outgrew the building in 1913, but owned it until 1961. The new owner had it stripped down to bare steel (3) and remodeled by the architectural descendants of the original designers, Cyrus L. W. Eidlitz and Andrew C. McKenzie. The bland effacement reopened in 1966.

Is its alteration really a loss? One thing worth remembering is that the building was a popular landmark for its entire life — very much so when it was built, but also years later, as picture postcards showed (2); it was clearly one of the

three or four New York buildings instantly recognizable to people all over the world. The building was not in itself remarkable — just another try at giving a skyscraper some fashion. The site had much to do with the Times Tower's conspicuousness. The *Times* chose it wisely, as the *Herald* had chosen their site elsewhere, a few years before. Both newspapers located buildings prominently in what was in each case the center of town at the time, where newspaper offices deserve to be (they are fortunate in having their names still associated with those central places). Seen this way, the Times Tower's new face and new use is clearly no improvement. What is now at No. 1 Times Square, on the Great White Way, at the Crossroads of the World, is not an important New York building, but only another piece of outdoor advertising — a junior-executive monument self-dedicated to "the show business of big business."

NEW YORK TELEPHONE COMPANY.   Only the ceiling remains in this shrine of instant communication, the Booth Room at the New York Telephone Company building. The directory altar and the booths like confessionals have given way to advanced equipment. The building, at 140 West Street, dates from 1923–26; McKenzie, Voorhees and Gmelin, architects.

CHRYSLER OBSERVATION LOUNGE.   Now housing television transmission equipment is the shell of what once was the Observation Lounge in the Chrysler building — the logically expressionistic summit of New York's most winning skyscraper. The vivid building by William Van Alen at Lexington Avenue and 42nd Street (where Edward Trumbull's lobby still remains) was completed in 1930.

BLACK, STARR & FROST. Like the Times Tower, the Black, Starr & Frost building (at the southwest corner of Fifth Avenue and 48th Street) has been transformed by the placement of a flashy new skin over the old skeleton. Unlike the Times Tower, the architecture destroyed in 1964 by the new owner, a bank on the make, was one of the best small business buildings in the city. It was designed in 1912 by Carrère and Hastings, architects of the New York Public Library.

LORD & TAYLOR, BROADWAY.   The Lord & Taylor department store occupied this now substantially altered building from 1872 to 1902, the fifth Manhattan location of the company. (The fourth was on Broadway and Grand Street.) This store was on the southwest corner of Broadway and 20th Street, and had an iron frame and a new steam elevator. The iron window walls of the building with their great areas of glass indicate how retail clothing was still something to be examined in the daylight.

1

55 WALL STREET. Isaiah Rogers built the Merchants Exchange (1) in 1836–42, on the site of an earlier one. It was distinguished by its Ionic colonnade and an eighty-foot dome. In 1863, the building became the Custom House, and the First National City Bank acquired it in 1899. By 1909, the bank had added four more stories by McKim, Mead and White. It had another giant order, Corinthian this time, piled over the sixteen Ionic columns — an original and staggering sight that can still be seen. Inside, an efficient pneumatic message system was installed (2). The new floors enclosed but at first did not cut off the original dome. Modifications were carried out to make the room a single banking floor (3), now altered and considerably diminished.

Very few institutional buildings on valuable land can be so efficient that they remain in successful use for 125 years. But this building's state of steady change through its history justifies calling it "lost," since it has come far from its greatest days — a fact that ought to be considered in the Preservation Commission's allowance for further change, now that 55 Wall Street has become a designated Landmark.

3

2

1

MARKETS AND SHOPS.   Retail marketing would undoubtedly account for the greatest turnover of money in New York, if it was considered a single industry. Shops therefore ought to have prominence in a book about a city, but the process of cash-and-carry is apparently so simple that its architecture is usually purely ornamental, besides being almost always ephemeral. A few to remember:

The vanished food market at Broadway and 95th Street (1), which somewhat resembled the earlier New Central Market, a free-enterprise grocery with rented stalls at Broadway and 48th Street, built in 1868 . . .

2

3

The Windsor Arcade (2), designed by Charles I. Berg for Elbridge Gerry, on the east side of Fifth Avenue between 46th and 47th Streets; New York's most famous and elaborate shopping block until it disappeared by halves in 1912 and 1920 . . . William Lamb's 1933–34 retail block at Madison Avenue, 59th to 60th Streets (3), where reflections of the International Style once could be discerned in the glass . . . And, of course, there are some shops in a retail chain's constant style that are remembered because they were around for so long (4).

4

PUBLIC
AMUSEMENTS.

The financial failures of New York's Freedomland and the 1964 World's Fair appear to indicate that this kind of outdoor amusement is no longer being supported by the public in numbers that justify the expense of their maintenance. Actually, the grand spectacle of middle-class society in general attendance at amusement parks and similar public recreation — the image of the Crystal Palace, the Columbian Exposition, the scenes painted by Manet, Seurat and Renoir — began to fade at the end of the 19th century. And this rapt public seems to have markedly diminished around the time when automobiles began to allow many people the privilege of seeking private amusements.

Yet it would be worth learning whether the automobile, as well as the television set and other vehicles of individual fancy, were really the cause of the decline of public amusements. Even after driving out into the natural landscape, most people today still seek the society of others. Picnic areas and comfortably tamed camping places are by far the most popular parts of national parks.

The reason for the decline of organized public amusements may have something to do with the modern status of children, and the place they have at the center of family life. If zoos, amusement parks and fairs — even museums — are seen as being principally for the entertainment of children, then what these have to offer adults must necessarily be limited. Old photographs of Luna Park and Dreamland have scarcely any children in them at all. The amusement parks were designed to be at their most magnificent at night. They were romantic environments where courtships could be forthrightly conducted. The Tunnels of Love were built for serious couples, not for bored children. Fun was a dignified adult proposition, and the present decline of public amusements may be principally the result of self-limitations — a diminished view of our own capacities.

The Coney Island Elephant was a well-known New York curiosity. Other houses shaped like elephants had been built in Europe. The beast's impressive architectural dimensions were noted on the reverse side of this advertising card. The Elephant, now long gone, also appears in a photo of Coney Island in King's 1893 *Handbook of New York City*.

THE CRYSTAL PALACE. The site of the New York Exhibition of 1853 was at Sixth Avenue and 42nd Street, just west of the Croton Reservoir. Schemes for an exhibition building submitted by Leopold Eidlitz and Bogardus & Hoppin were passed over in favor of an octagonal structure of iron and glass with a dome, by the architects George Carstensen and Charles Gildemeister (1). The Crystal Palace design was derivative of Paxton's 1851 London pavilion in name and materials, and both were also prefabricated, repetitive, and technologically precise. (The aerial view was made from the Latting

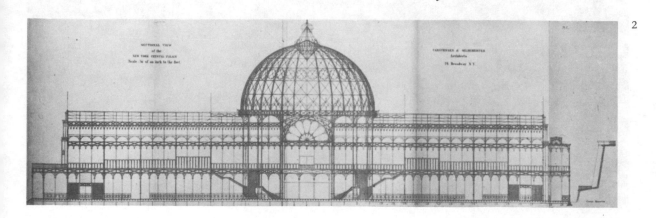

Observatory, a tall, braced-timber tower with an early steam elevator, built as a public attraction during the World's Fair. The tower stood across 42nd Street to the north, and burned down in 1856.)

Carstensen and Gildemeister's design (2) was perhaps unnecessarily complex and formally derivative, but for those very reasons it demanded sophisticated detailing and a great variety of framing techniques (3). While all this made it less interesting architecturally than the Crystal Palace in London, it was a widely publicized lesson to American designers in the versatile use of iron — a lesson soon transferred by others to theater roofs, skylights, train sheds, and blocks of iron buildings. There was a nationwide enthusiasm for the Crystal Palace and the possibilities of iron construction. Bogardus even thought iron buildings could be built ten miles high. Iron was a perfect material: strong, cheap, not easily rusted when cast, fireproof — or so it was thought. In fact, iron is drastically weakened in a high temperature.

The awful truth about iron and glass buildings became clear when the combustible contents of the Crystal Palace caught fire on October 5, 1858. The fire twisted and collapsed the entire structure in an incredible fifteen minutes' time. Soon after, the destruction of the Crystal Palace was being as widely vaunted as its creation (4).

3   4

CRYSTAL PALACE
RELICS !

Mrs. RICHARDSON, of New York, (who was one of the unfortunate persons burnt out by the fire that destroyed the Crystal Palace,) by permission of the MAYOR OF NEW YORK, and of JOHN H. WHITE, Esq., Crystal Palace Receiver, obtained a number of curiosities very valuable for a cabinet, produced by the melting of the Building, and articles on exhibition, which she now offers to visitors at the FAIR AT PALACE GARDEN, as interesting souvenirs of all that remains of the finest building ever erected in America—a building made entirely of glass and iron, except the floors—and supposed to be almost wholly free from danger of fire; yet, it was utterly destroyed on the 5th of October, 1858, in fifteen minutes' time. The evidence of the immense heat will be seen in the articles now offered for sale, as well worthy the attention of the curious.

An interesting memorial of the great Crystal Palace Exhibition, is found in Mrs. RICHARD-SON'S collection of Relics, which is on exhibition in the 2d floor. They consist of vitrified masses of glass, metals, &c., showing the intense heat which prevailed in the building at the time of its destruction.—Tax Sun, Oct. 11.

Wynkoop, Hallenbeck & Thomas, Printers, 113 Fulton Street, N. Y.

1

2

RECREATION PIERS.   The New York Regional Plan of
1929–31, a proposal that was not timid about its new highway plans for
Manhattan, nevertheless roundly disowned the West Side Highway. The
planners found fault with it because its location cut people off from the
Hudson River and made the development of new riverfront recreation facilities most difficult. The influence of the Regional Plan Association's comment
was presumably modest, because the alignment of the new East River Drive
soon repeated the mistake on the other side of the island. Since the penny-wise
New York commissioners who laid out the 1811 grid of streets had reasoned
that the city did not need many parks because of New York's healthful relationship with its river edges, one finds that official planning has, in its history,
both turned people toward the water and then stopped them from getting
there. This double bind may one day have to be resolved by means of expensive landfill and redevelopment.

Before Manhattan's girdling highways were built, and before pollution
devitalized the rivers, recreation piers provided some of New York's most
pleasant public playgrounds. The idea of recreation piers was a natural one
in Coney Island, where the now vanished Iron Pier at Brighton Beach was so
popular that it was featured in stereoscopic views (1, 2, 3). It was an I-shaped
construction with elaborate pavilions at both ends, and in addition to dining

4

and strolling, it was the landing place for the Iron Steamboats which brought holidaymakers there.

There were once six officially designated recreation piers in Manhattan, and one in Brooklyn — "Play Piers" as Jacob Riis called them, or "Roof Gardens" as the users did (4, 5). The first opened at the foot of East 3rd Street in 1897 at the instigation of Riis, and its enormous success led to others on the East River at 24th Street and 112th Street, and on the Hudson at Barrow Street (part of the Christopher Street Ferry slip), 50th Street and 129th Street. They were opened from 8:00 A.M. until 10:30 P.M. from June to November, and were crowded most of the day with children and later with parents and young couples, cool in the evening fresh river air.

5

STEEPLECHASE, THE FUNNY PLACE.   Steeplechase Park, created in 1897 as
the first of the great Coney Island amusement parks, closed for good in 1964, the twenty-five acre site
having been sold for a housing project. Steeplechase was "The Funny Place," as signboards used to say
(over the painted face of the founder George C. Tilyou wreathed in an incredible smile). The amusement
park got its name from one of its most famous rides — the wooden steeplechase horses that started together

1

at the top of a long system of track. Riders would mount the horses, each of which straddled one of the parallel rails. When the brake was removed, all the horses would start at once, zooming up and down the course that circled the pavilion and looped in and out through its walls (1, right). The building itself was a simple steel frame (2) housing, among other diversions, Coney Island's second most important Elephant (see page 181). The most popular attraction was the extra-cost Parachute Jump (1, left), a great draw at the time of the 1939 World's Fair. The park was once destroyed by fire in 1907, but was rebuilt in 1908. Mr. Tilyou meanwhile invited the public in to see the ruins for ten cents a look.

2

1

DREAMLAND.   The fantasy architecture of pleasure grounds might serve as a profitable source of information on the aspirations and imaginary adventures of a society. Once ordinary formalistic preconceptions are swept aside in the spirit of fun, design seems to turn directly toward the stuff of dreams inspired by contemporary ideals. (The Rhineland gardens of Schloss Schwetzingen had recreational "ruins" and a "mosque" in 1776, long before aspirations toward the Picturesque had made any inroads in serious German architecture.) Just as the amusement parks of today present as public fantasies strong images of space travel and scientific exploration, those of sixty years ago showed public fantasies common

to that time. New York had them in two prevailing moods: the Apollonian Luna Park, and the Dionysian Dreamland.

In Dreamland, long vanished, a culture that admired the work of the National Sculpture Society in Beaux-Arts triumphal arches found the lost world of legend — in forms not like Art Nouveau, as they might have been, but in decoration almost as original; and sometimes, as at the entrance facade, strangely Sullivanian (2). Stucco ornament illustrated fancies from Wagner (3) to *kitsch* (1). At night, bulbs would light the dragons' wings.

190

LUNA PARK. A mood and style at Coney Island which was far from spooky gorges — although with a prevailing fantasy of its own — was at Luna Park, beautiful Luna Park that the visiting Maxim Gorki called "fabulous beyond conceiving." Thompson and Dundy opened it in 1903, and the things it showed that had been borrowed from Chicago had nothing to do with Louis Sullivan. The great spectacle was the White City itself of the 1893 World's Fair, condensed (1) but also dematerialized (2). Like the White City (and the still extant Tivoli Gardens in Copenhagen), Luna Park was European, sophisticated, somehow noble; dignified fun. Before it burned down, it was a pleasure garden where ordinary people could savor amusements in good society, as at Vauxhall, Cremorne or the Bal Masqué.

1

2

WORLD'S FAIR 1939.   Returning from the 1937 Paris Exposition, Grover Whalen, president of the New York World's Fair Corporation, was optimistic on the subject of peace. Assuming that his prediction of the state of the world remained correct, he envisaged the opening of the World's Fair on April 30, 1939 on the theme of "Building the World of Tomorrow." World's fairs and national expositions present a situation where architecture is supposed to express national ambitions and ideals. In fact, those held since 1851, when international fairs were reinvented for post-classical times, have been basically celebrations of *laissez-faire* commerce and perpetually nineteenth-century ideas of trade and progress. In a depression year, Lewis Mumford called the notion of a fair a "completely tedious and unconvincing belief in the triumph of modern industry. The less said about *that* today, the better."

But the biggest and costliest of all fairs up until that time opened as scheduled, and perhaps even many of the nation's 13,000,000 unemployed passed through the turnstiles where the pre-pop art National Cash Register building, designed by Walter Dorwin Teague (1), busily counted the customers. Once on the reclaimed land of Flushing Meadows, where 6,700,000 cubic yards of garbage had been moved and graded in 190 days, visitors could see and orient themselves from the Trylon and Perisphere (2), the theme centerpiece by Wallace K. Harrison and J. André Fouilhoux. This was a 700 foot high tapered pillar (the "finite") and a 200 foot steel-framed globe (the "infinite" — or was it the other way around?). Between the two was the Helicline: a ramp. At night, moving colored marble patterns were projected on the globe. Color was in fact one of the significant design preoccupations of the Fair, where the Board of Design (which made sure, among other things, that state pavilions were stylistically correct in deriving from Georgian, French or Spanish influence) had Julian E. Garnsey, for the sake of good taste, select 499 colors available to architects.

In the spirit of the Big Cash Register, there were pavilions for Cosmetics (a giant lady's powder box), RCA (a radio tube), Gas (grid points on a range surrounding a flame), and the Continental Baking Company (a doughnut). In the midst of all this highly finite design soared the infinite Finnish Pavilion (3, 4), Alvar Aalto the architect, fresh from attaining his new world reputation in the 1937 Paris Exposition. Aalto's three-story undulating screen repeated the vertical stick idea that was common to his 1937 and 1938 pavilions in Paris and Lapua, Finland. While the representation being made in New York was not specifically of forestry and agriculture, the theme of his historic design at Lapua, the technical performance clearly evoked some associations with Finnish lakes and forests. The physical impact was apparently

1

2

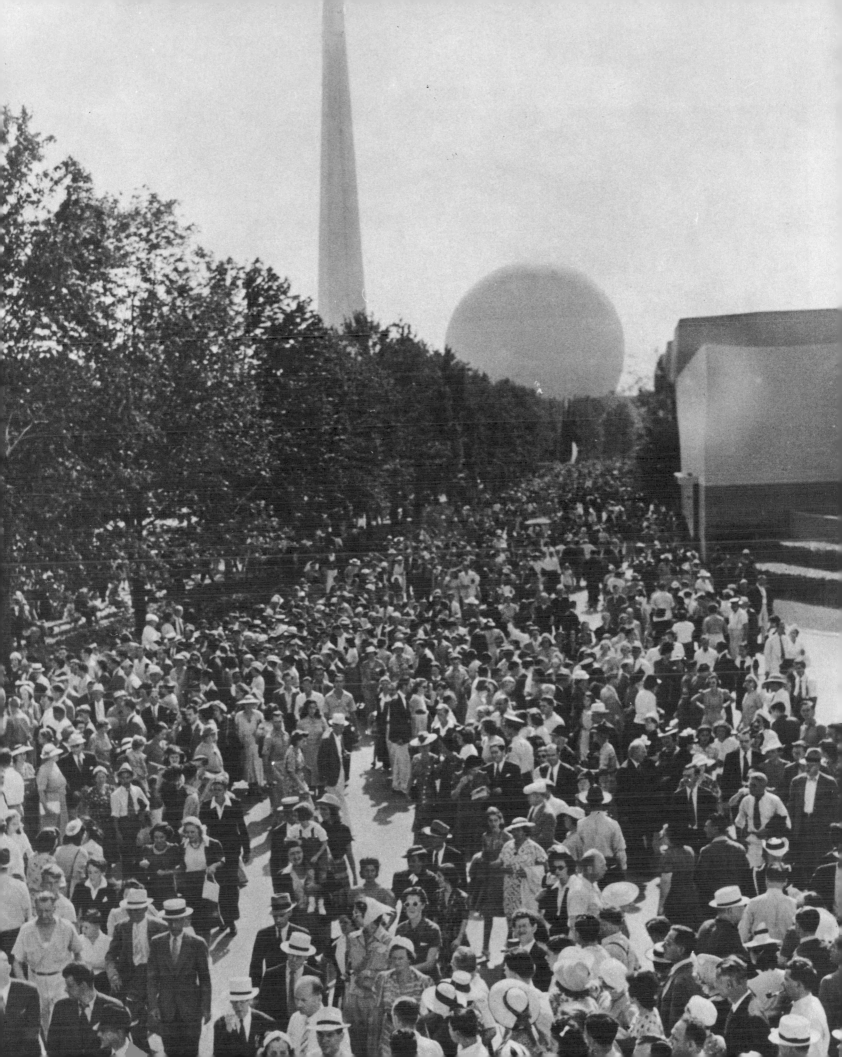

3

even more evocative. Siegfried Giedion found that "The cantilever of the upper stories, which so intensifies the impression of hovering movement, provides room for a concentrated display of objects. The outstanding feature is the new modeling of inner space that is involved in this experiment, which to many still appears rude and almost barbaric." The loss of the Finnish Pavilion at the end of the Fair is comparable to the loss of Mies van der Rohe's German Pavilion in Barcelona, built ten years earlier. Both were irreplaceable landmarks of modern architecture.

Next to the Finnish Pavilion, some of the few other good works at the 1939 Fair seem small losses, if otherwise deserving of credit. The Danish unit of the Hall of Nations (5) had some of the same crisp design as the

4

Museum of Modern Art (see page 109), finished the same year. The French Pavilion (6) had lots of character, and even style, though transitional.

The New York 1939 Fair first showed to the world some lasting innovations, if not any as revolutionary as the use of neon lighting in the Chicago Fair of 1933. Some of these were the exhibits that moved to the audience (and vice versa), the effective and wide use of mirrors, and the telephone exhibit, where free long-distance calls could be made before an appreciative audience. What these novelties had in common was the participating crowd, the people who were there to see. In retrospect, the Board of Design's layout for the Fair (7) was unexceptionable and the Fair's architectural mean was probably higher than that of Manhattan, but the discovery that people were what exhibits

5   6

were for was the most significant contribution. In the *Architectural Record* in 1940, a writer looked back and thought that this proved "an influence toward democracy more powerful than many a columned building." A more distant view adds the ideas of the Road of Tomorrow to the Fair's prescience — only twenty years after, the highway had already changed the nation even more than anyone had dared predict. Probably most people remembered best General Motors and Ford, and Pierre Labatut's fireworks displays — "the nearest approach to chaos that man can contrive for purposes of sheer entertainment." Before the Fair closed, Grover Whelan found man approaching chaos for other purposes.

7

WORLD'S FAIR 1964.   The Board of Design of the 1939 World's Fair saw to it that the improved fairgrounds would be able to remain as a park. The site plan, the work of many men, had been designed with a view to Lewis Mumford's suggestion that an ideal scheme was one giving the visitor an immediate understanding of the whole exposition. The result was a rigid pattern where axes crossed more or less concentric rings. Even on the ground, it was a paper plan; absolutely two-dimensional despite the opportunities presented by all the earth-moving that had to be done. But once the Trylon and Perisphere formed a center to the ring avenues and radial avenues, the plan at least heeded Mumford. The central symbol was as directional as a north arrow, and told the visitor where he was.

When the site was used again for the 1964 World's Fair (after a term as a neglected park, and for a while as the United Nations location) the theme symbol again occupied the center, but the Unisphere was just the opposite of a directional guide. A banal and sculpturally crude globe based on an armillary sphere, the skeleton structure of hoops looked and worked exactly like the celestial globes it was patterned after. It was something to look through; and from any radial avenue, the symbol looked the same and failed to be a guide.

In the sense that the Unisphere never satisfied a useful purpose, it was truly symbolic of the 1964 Fair. A dismally unimaginative and uncomprehending management caused the resignation of its consulting architects and financial advisors. Most foreign countries stayed officially out because the Bureau of International Expositions had withheld recognition. The exposition run by Robert Moses and his staff hardly bore any relation to its avowed theme, "Peace Through Understanding." In fact, as a representation of international, national, or even civic ideals and ambitions, it seemed so bankrupt that its generous support with public funds was virtually a public embarrassment. Amid all the crassness and chaos, the inference was — as Yale Professor Vincent Scully described it in a review for *Life* magazine — that this was all accurate, it was America, that Mr. Moses had our number.

2

3

4

Within the organizational shambles, many individual works were witless and savage, the average architectural accomplishment being far lower than that of 1939. There were, of course, Gulliverian exhibits, such as the U.S. Rubber tire (1), which George Washington Gale Ferris would hardly recognize as related to his trim invention of 1893. The most enthusiastic attendance was at the Belgian Village (2, 3) — an artificial bit of Tiny Europe, where the popularity of its make-believe streets only indicated how incoherent the rest of the Fair was.

What the Fair really had to offer (with one exception) was not architecture, at least not in the old sense of the word — not buildings. It offered exhibits, usually wholly internal presentations, some of them excellent. The pretentious shapes given the pavilions seldom had any relation to what went on inside. While the architecture provided competing fancy forms, the whole nature of exposition spectacle had changed with film experiments, moving displays, moving audiences. Some exceptional experiences were offered at the IBM, General Motors and Johnson Wax pavilions. The best thing the Fair had, however, was a distinguished work of architecture that would have been outstanding in any company: the New York State Pavilion, which somehow captured, without belittling, the spirit of public assembly for entertainment: a walk-in, walk-out canopy connected to observation towers (4); for all its decoration and high style, truly a "less is more" pronouncement. We are indebted to architect Philip Johnson and Governor Nelson Rockefeller for this affirmation of people's importance amid denial and doubt. The bare structure still remains standing, and a new practical use would be good news.

IN MEMORIAM.

New York is not young as cities go, though its reputation for newness (even its name) makes us discount that. Its old buildings are as venerable as some of the oldest that remain in other great cities, which is vaguely reassuring. Plainly, however interested we are in the future, we remain decisively attached to the past we leave behind. "Nostalgia" is our unsatisfactory term for it.

The word in English is hopelessly wishy-washy. It seems to denote something between a handwring and a tearjerk, referring as it does to wistful, regretful feelings. Nowadays most urban dwellers accept that a city's past vitalizes a coherent sense of the present, but calling that "nostalgia" evokes the approximate reaction that one would get from mentioning heirlooms or embroidery. My original Preface of 1967 wondered whether there was more to nostalgia than sentimental longing. The strength of feeling provoked me. It seemed a psychologically profound impulse of some importance, and I knew I should say more.

The aesthetician Adrian Stokes provides a useful lead. Stokes, perhaps best known for his assertion that "architecture is limited to forms without events" (which out of context seems to glorify the position of the detached onlooker contemplating the purely visual), elsewhere more essentially tells us that architecture "draws upon the origin of all sense of wholeness."* The latter seems to me exactly correct. For Stokes, "wholeness" is a longed-for and nearly overpowering psychological objective. It is an involved appreciation shared by both users and observers of architecture. I infer that the wholeness he means includes not only the practical and anthropological signals we derive from architectural form, proportion, space, figure, line and mass, but the acute longing for a familiar sight that we sometimes describe as nostalgia. I'd take that a step further: what we look for is not a familiar sight restored (for which a crafty reconstruction might do), but one whose genuinely continuous existence serves to guarantee our sense of Platonic wholeness, philosophical analogy, personal connection, security and belonging. If that is indeed what we draw upon, we can reliably feel that our nostalgia for certain buildings and places amounts to nothing less than the quality of remembrance and belonging that we become half lost without.

The first edition of this book contained a chapter entitled "Landmarks in Danger." Thirty-four years later it is possible to resolve the suspense. Buildings which appeared there that still remain today are the Friends Meeting House on 20th Street (not redeveloped); Madison Square Park (not undermined by an underground garage); most of Broome and Grand Streets, the Haughwout & Co. store on Broadway, and the little Singer building at Prince Street (none of them laid waste by Robert Moses's potentially destructive Lower Manhattan Expressway proposal, which was finally stopped); the J. P. Morgan residence on Madison Avenue and 37th Street (not demolished by its previous owners); the Jackson Square Library (though it's no longer a library); the Hall of Records at Chambers and Centre streets and the Custom House at Bowling Green (both of which have some new uses); and Sailors' Snug Harbor on Staten Island.

The buildings from that chapter that are gone are Ernest Flagg's Singer Tower, the Bogardus Laing Stores, the Ziegfeld Theater, the Astor Hotel and the old Metropolitan Opera. They appear here with

---

* In *Smooth and Rough*, London, 1951. To refute the narrow notion that "architecture is limited to forms without events," I'd suggest considering the absurdity of trying to appraise the architectural space shown on the cover in disregard of its events, persons and their emotions.

a few further pictures. Though the Seventh Regiment Armory shell lives on, its contents have been substantially altered, so that is included, as are a few new lost subjects. Ellis Island's future was in doubt in 1967, but it has now partially become a museum. (As the home of strong memories, it is in the final chapter, "Places and Moments.")

I have included no new "Landmarks in Danger" chapter. A New York friend wryly told me in 1999 that nothing was in danger except from the preservation movement itself. He was probably thinking about the dilatory endgames of the Laing Stores, the old Met and the Rivoli movie palace. His wisecrack notwithstanding, it is clear that urban losses have accumulated since the 1960s because New York has continued to evolve, and we'll never outrun present and future "dangers" that concern many.

Frankly, I've left out threatened buildings because including some would increase the number of unarguably worthy subjects for this book to consider. My shortlist for these two new chapters was finally achieved with the judicious application of a radically subjective standard: what some aspect of lost New York had to do with me. By producing some dimensions of meaning that I can vouch for, I can at least lay claim to some internally structured objectivity. This strikes me as the best practical way to deal with problems arising from — as Richard Goldstein put it in the *Village Voice* — "the chronic sensation that the world I know is missing from the world I see."

A 1967 photo from the Danny Lyon series "The Destruction of Lower Manhattan" records the demolition of 82 Beekman Street — a humanistic and innovative cast-iron-clad building sacrificed, with others, for a traffic scheme. The wanton destruction was justified as "slum clearance." James Bogardus built 82 Beekman Street in 1853 for Tatham & Brothers.

THE FARCICAL END OF BOGARDUS'S LAING STORES.　　In 1849 James Bogardus finished this four-story row of storehouses for Edgar H. Laing, some time before his own Eccentric Mill Works (see page 166) was completed.　The Laing Stores — erected in two months — was not a complete iron structure such as those Bogardus and Daniel Badger separately fabricated later.　It was valuable because it had a historically early iron-clad exterior and was the only complete building by Bogardus that survived in New York.

The first edition of this book noted that the building was "slated for demolition, but with the cooperation of other city departments, the Landmarks Preservation Commission has succeeded in saving most of the iron facades.　They will be taken down and preserved for re-erection on a future site."　What actually happened was that the Landmarks Commission stored the 150 tons of cast-iron elements in a vacant lot in lower Manhattan, where thieves were caught stealing the last pieces in June 1974.　The rest had been sold for scrap.　The fifty-nine panels recovered were moved to an empty building uptown, but in June 1977 it was discovered that these, too, had been stolen.　Mocked by all, the chairman of the Landmarks Commission wrote to the *New York Times* blaming everyone else for not taking historical preservation seriously because public indignation was greater about the thefts than the demolition. Sadly, the Commission's neglect was what proved terminal.

202

1

2

THE ELITE SEVENTH REGIMENT'S ARMORY. The Seventh Regiment Armory, between Park and Lexington Avenues, 66th to 67th Streets, has been sporadically modified for more modern military uses than mustering and drill and for other social purposes (latterly, a performance space in the old drill hall). The regiment was once a local militia largely recruited from the social elite, though not when I drilled there in the early 1960s. After the Seventh did its bloody best in the 1849 Astor Place riot and distinguished itself in the 1863 Civil War draft riots, a public subscription was raised for the privately owned armory, built 1877–1880 by Clinton and Russell, architects, and Charles MacDonald, engineer, who for the first time adapted the structure of the train shed for the regiment's drill hall. The exterior isn't much changed except for the loss of a spire on the central tower, but the fine interiors — now substantially altered — included the main staircase (2), company rooms and the restored Veterans' Room (1). The latter, with the library, was decorated by the Associated Artists collaboration, which included Louis Comfort Tiffany and Stanford White. It was one of the nation's best buildings of the decade.

1

2

THE GRAND, JEFFERSON, HIPPODROME & ZIEGFELD.

Some theaters deserve to be commemorated for their very special attractions. New York's Yiddish theater — as two of my grandparents fondly recounted — arose as immigrants populated the neighborhood from Broome and Grand Streets to the Bowery and Second Avenue, which already held some theaters. A memorable one was the vanished three-gallery Grand Theatre on the Bowery (1). It was used by the actor-manager Jacob Adler for the production of artistically serious works such as the Yiddish *King Lear* shown on the marquee in the Byron photograph of 1905 (2).

By then the English-language theaters had begun to move uptown. The Jefferson opened in 1913 at the height of the vaudeville era. It was on 13th Street between Second and Third Avenues, with a main entrance passage through the block to the more desirable and accessible 14th Street (4). After it became linked to the big-time Keith circuit in 1920, its players included the Marx Brothers, Mae West, Jack Benny and Fred Allen. "The Jefferson was considered the toughest house in New York," says George Burns in his book *Gracie*. "It was where bookers from every agency came to look at acts." It was a movie house from the '30s to the '60s and was finally demolished in 1999.

The New York Hippodrome (3), which opened in 1905 on Sixth Avenue between 43rd and 44th Streets, was the work of theatrical impresario cum architectural designer Frederick Thompson with Elmer

3

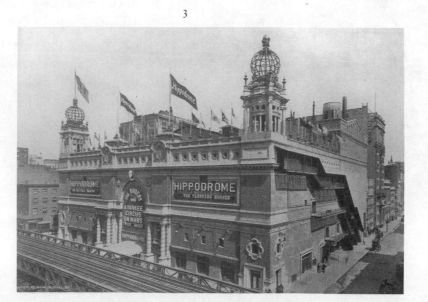

4

5

Lundy, who also created Coney Island's Dreamland and Luna Park (pages 189–91). Extravagantly multi-bulbed in the early days of electrification, its theatrical space of 5,300 seats was then called the largest in the world. The Hippo's decorative plasterwork abounded with exotic fauna; the thrust stage platform held two circus rings and an apron that was submersible in a large water tank where naval pageants were held and where Annette Kellerman, "the million dollar mermaid," could swim about. It was substantially redecorated in 1935 for the Billy Rose production of Rodgers and Hart's *Jumbo*, which starred Jimmy Durante, Paul Whiteman's orchestra, aerial acts and an elephant; but as Richard Rodgers says in his autobiography, "Billy Rose had a vision that far exceeded his finances." The production closed in five months, and the colorful but insupportable Hippodrome survived only another four years. The wacky, classical expressionist Ziegfeld Theater (5), at the northwest corner of Sixth Avenue and 54th Street — completed in 1927, demolished in 1966 — was the Hearst-financed work of the Viennese-born stage designer–architect Joseph Urban, assisted by Thomas W. Lamb. Behind its bulging, posterlike front, intended to express a sort of Ziegfeld Folly in stone, it had a smoothly elliptical domed auditorium encircled by a mural billed as "the world's largest oil painting" (*Joy of Life* by Lillian Gaertner). Upstairs in a memorious room (6), Mr. Ziegfeld was able to see his remarkable business associates (left to right, Jack Donahue, Marilyn Miller, George Gershwin, Sigmund Romberg, Flo Ziegfeld).

6

THE MAGNIFICENT OLD MET.   The Met was the archetype of unjustified destruction in cities: a great public building at the disposal solely of its owner — a cultural management board at that. The principal reason for the demolition of the Broadway and 39th Street Metropolitan Opera House was the Metropolitan Opera Association's refusal to spare it for fear of competition from another opera company using their old house. They sold the opera property several years ahead of time with compulsory demolition written into the bill of sale, and also managed to convince the Landmarks Preservation Commission, the City Council and some New York music critics that conservation of the old house would hurt opera in New York. Would that have proved true? A generation later, to a culture that now can't get enough opera, it's obvious how foolishly shortsighted such monopoly protection was. But it was plain even then. Without Landmarks Commission support, New York mounted only ad hoc protest. The Met's officers successfully overwhelmed a clear city planning issue with a clamor of scorn and impudent claims (among them the demand for a triple payoff from citizens trying to buy back the building), while posing as friends of art. The important planning issue, never heard over Met president Anthony Bliss's fortissimo, was the question of where official culture should live: exclusively in a center or more widely across the city. New York badly needed the anchor of a cultural institution below Times Square that might have become a Redoutensaal or Opéra de la Bastille, or even the home of a new Hammerstein's Manhattan Opera. In January 1967 the roof came off the 39th Street building that would have most adequately and economically served such a purpose. The Met, usually with capacity audiences, couldn't afford competition, and New York couldn't afford anything but free-enterprise opera.

1

2

Some defend the demolition with the claim that the old building was badly in need of redecoration and technical improvement, so what was really lost? Well, to start with, a majestic and glamorous auditorium. And then there was its history, touched on in the next chapter.

The old Met opened in 1882 with an auditorium that held 3,045 and the largest stage in America, defeating the rest of the field (see page 79); it was rebuilt in 1893 after a fire, and got a new proscenium in 1905 (2). The architect of the dignified building (1) was Josiah Cleveland Cady, and the rebuilt auditorium (3) was one of the liveliest achievements of the New York Public Library architects Carrère and Hastings. In 1940 extra seats were gained by turning boxes in the second tier into a gallery (see cover).

3

1

GENTLEMEN'S AND LADIES' CLUBS.   In an age when club membership was virtually a social requirement for men and sometimes women of nearly every ethnic group, business purpose and economic class, the Union League, formed by Republicans during the Civil War, was one of the most prominent. Its third clubhouse (now gone), a competition-winner by the Boston firm of Peabody & Stearns, was completed in 1881 at the northeast corner of Fifth Avenue and 39th Street. The 1886 photograph (1) appeared in the *American Architect and Building News*, which brushed aside the architectural prize by unkindly describing the building's somewhat busy expression as "the negation of repose."

Scores and scores of New York clubs were built between the Civil War and World War I. Many were architecturally distinguished, and most have now vanished. The cylindrically bayed Women's City Club (2) was photographed in 1910. Its street address and other information remain obscure, but it seems certain that the building has disappeared, since such memorably *mouvementé* architecture would be celebrated now.

2

THE WELL-DISPOSED ASTOR HOTEL.   To the sojourner in the city — by which I mean a teenager in about 1950 such as me — the Astor's most attractive quality was that it was a large, dignified, socially appealing building that reigned over Times Square, providing a respite from the otherwise continuous perceptual clamor that surrounded it. (The neighboring and similarly imposing Knickerbocker and Rector hotels were already gone.) In their historically themed bedrooms with windows that had close-up views of New York's bull's-eye, its guests no doubt agreed — including Cole Porter's character "Mimsy Starr / Who got pinched in the Astor Bar! Well, did you evah?" Sadly, Mimsy lost her hangout in the mid-'60s because the Astor's large site, an obvious real estate bull's-eye, presented the opportunity of being acquired through a single property deal. The hotel should have remained where it belonged.

The Astor, on Broadway between 44th and 45th Streets, where Times Square narrows (see page 230), was designed by Clinton and Russell. Its main section was completed in 1904, four years before the New York to Paris Automobile Race whose start is shown in the photo. For a while it boasted one of New York's most popular roof gardens for dining in the open air. Roof gardens were great attractions in the years before the city had practical widespread air conditioning and before urban traffic noise and fumes became discouraging.

LEVERAGED BUYOUT ON WALL STREET.   The debonair twenty-story tower
topped by a lantern and cupola, seen to the right of the classical portico of the New York Stock
Exchange, was the Gillender Building at the corner of Wall and Nassau Streets. Built in 1897, it lasted
only a bit more than twelve years — probably the shortest life of any tall building in New York — before
being torn down to provide part of the site for the thirty-nine-story Bankers Trust Building. Mrs.
Helena L. Gillender Asinari received $1,500,000 for the fugacious structure, which took thirty-five days
to demolish in 1910, a worthy subject for newspaper reports, as not many steel buildings had so far been
razed. The steel was recycled, the decorative plaster interiors sold to dealers, and the exterior granite
reground for use as tombstones at Green-Wood Cemetery in Brooklyn.

1

2

THE ELEVATED RAILWAY.   New York's initial response to London's pioneering underground railways was to figure that elevating them would be cheaper. The first in New York, the West Side and Yonkers Patented Railway, was a cable-traction line built from 1867 to 1870 along Greenwich Street. Within a few years the means of locomotion had become steam engines; there were elevated structures for miles along Second, Third, Sixth and Ninth Avenues; and separate sections were being built in the Bronx and Brooklyn. The economic advantages of rapid transit were so manifest that little attention was paid at first to adjacent occupiers, whose air was besmoked, streets beshadowed (2; the visual bewilderment below was exploited in the car chase of the 1971 film *The French Connection*), and shaken buildings bedighted with black ironwork. Though some of the elaborately roofed overhead stations had charm, they darkened streets even more (1, the 32nd Street Greeley Square station of the Sixth Avenue El). After the first subway was finished in 1904, the demolition of the elevated railways slowly gave back Manhattan's streets and avenues. Today most are gone except in the outer boroughs.

1

THE SINGER TOWER, TALLEST IN THE WORLD.   Ernest Flagg's impressive design of the little Singer building on Broadway at Prince Street, which survives, led to his commission for the forty-seven-story Singer Tower at 149 Broadway at Liberty Street. It was the tallest building in the world from 1908 until the completion of the Metropolitan Life Tower eighteen months later. The tower's projecting attic floors, mansarded roof and lantern long remained a characteristic figure in the New York skyscape (see page 254). The shaft rose above the lower section — a building stage that had been completed earlier — with an unprecedented slenderness (1), braced by crossed diagonals in the corners, a kind of support against wind pressure now commonly used in steel buildings. The demonstration of a tall tower limited to a quarter of the site area influenced New York's 1916 zoning ordinance. The form of Flagg's tower top, and the materials of his extroverted lobby of colored marble, bronze and glass saucer-domes (2), reflected some of the stylistic preoccupations of his training at the École des Beaux-Arts in Paris. But the main exogenous inspiration seems to have been the client's product: that ornamental, practical, technologically advanced turn-of-the-century Singer sewing machine, whose logo even appeared on the lobby capitals. The building was demolished in 1966 to clear the site for a bulkier and higher one, and achieved another first: the first widely recognized former "tallest" to bite the dust.

212

ROTHAFEL'S ROXY & LOEW'S AUTHENTIC PARADISE.   The answer to "What's playin' at the Roxy?" has been sweet nothing since 1961, when Samuel L. ("Roxy") Rothafel's 6,200-seat "Cathedral of the Motion Picture," built in 1927 (1), was added to the scrap heap of history. It joined midtown's other former movie palaces the Strand ("In a Class by Itself," built 1914, demolished 1987), the Criterion (the original of that name, 1914–1936), the Rialto ("the Temple of the Motion Picture," 1916–1998), the Rivoli (the original with a Parthenon pediment, 1917–1932), the Capitol (1919–1972), the Loew's State (built 1921, divided 1968, demolished 1986), and the Paramount (1926–1967).   The Roxy remained in blood-stirring high function when I sat with a classmate in the first row to see the premier CinemaScope film *The Robe* (1953), hearing an unprecedentedly stereophonic

2

"Hail Caesar!" from our extreme left and "Hail to thee!" from somewhere behind our necks. Now the name of Roxy has ascended to join Astor and Ritz and Delmonico as one of the limited number of classy handles that will ever after be borrowed for the likes of delicatessens, dry cleaners and soubrettes.

What were these showplaces? Historically the "movie palace" was a unique building type that evolved largely from Rothafel's idea of transforming the nickelodeon into a temple of splendor and sumptuous comfort where screen, stage and musical entertainments of considerable size might appear. The midtown movie palaces were all built during the silent era, when film audiences could be substantially boosted by music and supporting stage attractions. The movie palace's greatest manifestation occurred naturally in New York, where the film studios had their financial and administrative headquarters, the media were most concentrated, and long booking engagements were potent enough as advertisements to countenance some financial running losses. And the showplaces were preponderantly tied to the studios, which is why *The Robe*, a 20th Century Fox film, opened at the Roxy. The era of movie palace building was brief — from the pioneering uptown Regent Theater in 1913 through the climax of the Roxy Theater itself in 1927, and a few spectacular sunset years in the early 1930s. The greatest makers were Roxy Rothafel, an impresario-stagecraftsman born in Minnesota, and John Eberson, an architect-decorator born in Vienna and trained in Dresden.

A former nickelodeon owner, Rothafel took on management of the 116th Street Regent in 1913. Applying new ideas such as altering the stage and seating pitch, lowering the projection booth and training uniformed ushers to perform like the Marine he himself had been, he went on to plan the midtown Strand with architect Thomas Lamb, specifying every visual, spatial and execution requirement. Rothafel and Lamb continued developing the movie palace form in the midtown Rialto and the Rivoli (and Lamb was used by others on the Capitol and Loew's State). Challenged by the grand size and opulence of the Capitol and the Paramount, Roxy engaged a Chicago architect, Walter W. Ahlschlager, to help beget the great palace that bore his name. The site was a huge jagged diagonal between 50th and 51st Streets and Sixth and Seventh Avenues, which had formerly held a car barn.

When the Roxy opened, Ahlschlager told the souvenir program writer that his architectural and decorative approach was "a maximum use of restraint and negation." That was rubbish, since the Roxy's color and ornament were red plush and bronze Late Baroque–San Simeon. And of course the scale was immense. The building could contain nearly 10,000 people at one time, including standees, lobby queues, staff,

4

orchestra and performers. The main truss, "the largest ever fabricated," weighed 210 tons. One of the sub-departments was the music library, planned before Vitagraph sound, which contained 10,000 selections and 50,000 orchestrations that had been bought from Victor Herbert (though I recall hearing mostly "Night on Bald Mountain" and "The Skater's Waltz"). The organ chamber was 13 by 18 by 60 feet, with 8-by-60-foot tone openings. The auditorium's "Deagan Chimes," twenty-one belfry bells, were behind movable shutters to control the immense volume of sound. With the Roxy launched, Rothafel moved on to his final triumph, fathering Radio City Music Hall with Rockefeller Center's team of modernist architects.

My highest aesthetic experience in movie palace architecture, though, occurred closer to home: at the Loew's Paradise (2–5) between the Grand Concourse and Creston Avenue at 184th–188th Streets in the Bronx, built in 1929 after movie palaces had saturated the Times Square area. (The big neighborhood movie palaces were built after the silent era, but they saved on the costs of stage productions then less commercially necessary by using touring shows from the midtown palaces.) The 3,885-seat Paradise was the sovereign achievement of the great John Eberson, deviser of the "atmospheric" movie house of polychromed plaster and illusionistic lighting effects, who later decorated Thomas Lamb's 1932 Loew's 72nd Street (pages 84–85).

Within the Paradise, one proceeded through space after space contemplating Baroque fragments, Rococo cartouches and grilles, aedicules, careening putti, flower garlands, draperies, cypress gardens, mechanical birds and plaster copies of European sculptures, including a Medici duke by Michelangelo. In the auditorium these were bathed in slowly changing colored lights under a moving cloud-scudded sky and twinkling stars, all presenting an alternative to watching the film that was well worth considering.

The provenance of such architectural scenography became plain to me several years later when I studied Baroque architecture in Eberson's homelands and was able to mull over the efforts of J. Dientzenhofer in Austria, the Asam brothers in Bavaria, and M. D. Poppelmann in Dresden. In a manner that I remembered first seeing at the Loew's Paradise, some of the Baroque masters' religious designs were blissfully invasive polychromed sculptural dioramas magically lit, presenting alternatives to following the Mass that churchgoers had no doubt found well worth considering for 250 years. Tragically, in an industry with no further need for secular transfigurations, the Paradise was progressively altered, then gutted in 1973; it lasted only 44 years.

5

The movie palaces' ultimate fates and terminal dates were kindly investigated by Christopher Gray of the Office for Metropolitan History.

216

ROBERT MOSES'S RUINS. Moses's biographer Robert A. Caro equivocates about his subject's contributions: "Would New York have been a better place to live if Robert Moses had never built anything? Would it have been a better city if the man who shaped it had never lived? . . . It is impossible to say."

Perhaps Caro, in his estimable work *The Power Broker,* falls for the great-man fallacy, which holds that certain territories never would have been claimed if the great man hadn't come along. All one can truly say is that Moses clearly got there first. The parks, bridges and highways he rapidly achieved, to the near-unanimous praise of editors and lending institutions and the near-unanimous silence of crushed members of the public, might have been attained by others — only more patiently and sensitively, with less police power and automobile preference and with tens of thousands fewer eminent-domain evictions. A great man? Well, in and around New York Robert Moses built a lot. He also destroyed a lot. Most of Moses's career was as the appointed head of multiple quangos, the British acronym for "quasi-autonomous non-governmental organizations" — such as his main fiefdom, the Triborough Bridge and Tunnel Authority. There he reigned supreme without democratic review, since the political value of a quango is that it wields official power with impunity. Moses wielded it efficiently, powerfully and self-righteously. In the sizable archive of photographs preserved by his quango of Moses opening "improvements" and receiving tributes, no picture seems more unwittingly telling than the one of him exchanging a congratulatory glad-hand with Generalísimo Francisco Franco (1).

A conspicuous Moses contribution was the New York Coliseum, where I once had the psychic misfortune to work in an office for a couple of years. Apart from its having originated in a typically questionable creative dip into public finances, it was perhaps the stiffest and surliest prominent modern building in New York (2, seen in the form of an anniversary cake that Robert Moses is dishing out to supportive bankers), with a relationship to its Columbus Circle context that was disrespectful to the site and to its users. According to the opening press release, "the clean, sharp lines of the attractive new structure, conservatively styled," merely replaced a "drab collection of rundown buildings which were cleared from the site." That kiss-off can be weighed by comparing the Coliseum, even in sugary cake form, with a demolition photo of the previous buildings on the site that it succeeded (3), which, though modest, were congenial and inoffensive.

The Coliseum appears in this chapter because its passing (which seems imminent as this is written) is one loss to remember with gratitude. I'll welcome the gradual replacement of many other Moses-built achievements with more sensitive and graceful ones and the eventual eradication of his name from others. For a start, we could give a new name to the Robert Moses Causeway, his gratuitous bridge for cars to Fire Island, one of the places that would have been destroyed had he succeeded in running a highway through it. The No Good Causeway, perhaps.

1

2

3

PLACES & MOMENTS.

1

The intersection between a given place and a given time is an exact point. That's why people remember, as if it were significant, where they were when they heard about President Kennedy's death and the weather on the day their first child was born. There ought to be a word for such nodes of importance, but I don't believe Kurt Vonnegut has thought of one yet. A *tockstead*, shall we say?

Tocksteads actually needn't be perfectly exact, only perfectly telling. Like the *Daily News* photo of John Lennon outside the Dakota a few months before he was murdered there (1) or the posed picture of uncomfortable-looking customers' men around a stock ticker at a Wall Street brokerage in early 1929 (2). A tockstead, or whatever one chooses to call it, is the four-dimensional setting for an epiphany, an event elucidated by a realization. Such as the appearance of an old minimalism at the Fourth of July 1976 Bicentennial — the functional clarity of tall sailing ships — against the new minimalism of the geometrical-looking World Trade Center and the flat landfill for Battery Park City (3). Or the patient porters at the arrivals carriageway of Pennsylvania Station, waiting forever for the next taxi that will never come down that vanished ramp (4).

As I have the impure view that architecture has to be event-linked and emotion-linked to be entirely appreciated, I treasure the memorable tocksteads of the metropolitan space-time continuum (though "places and moments" may sufficiently describe them). They can be painfully missed or yearningly re-imagined, even if some of the buildings remain.

2

3

4

NEW YORK GOES WILD

Clearly New Yorkers have it in them to go wild, but since the Astor Place riot of May 10, 1849, and the draft riots of July 13–16, 1863, bloodshed usually hasn't accompanied most crowd demonstrations and countervailing forces. Of those that follow, some were ominous; others were more benign manias at sporting events.

1

THOMSON REWRITES HISTORY AT THE POLO GROUNDS. This magical photo (1) of the Polo Grounds at its peak moment on October 3, 1951, remains with us, unlike the talismanic home run ball itself, whose subsequent possession is shrouded in mystery and raises profound questions in Don DeLillo's 1997 novel *Underworld* ("He's after the baseball now and there's no time to ask himself why"). Bobby Thomson is slugging the homer that reversed the ending of the game to win the National League playoff for the New York Giants against the Brooklyn Dodgers, shown against the grandstand where the ball landed, dotted line helpfully provided by the New York *Daily News*. A rabid Giants fan until baseball paled for me when the team left New York in 1957, I watched it happen on television. No decent photos exist of Thomson rounding the bases since the crowd was, well, going wild. They mobbed the infield.

In the view from the air (2), the Polo Grounds, demolished in 1964 to make way for a housing development, is in Manhattan in the foreground, with the still extant Yankee Stadium in the distance on the Bronx side of the river. Thomson's achievement was the Polo Grounds' supreme moment because it was the climax of the 1951 climb by the Giants, managed by Leo Durocher, to the top of the league, one of the most dramatic advances by a team in baseball history. As the Woody Allen character says in his 1997 film *Deconstructing Harry*, "When he hit that home run it was the only hint I had that there may be a God."

2

1

ROBINSON STEALS HOME; L.A. STEALS DODGERS. Jackie Robinson was
the player who singly personified the Brooklyn Dodgers and their home stadium, Ebbets Field (1). Until
Robinson, professional baseball had kept black players in a separate and unequal minor league of their own.
Robinson was the player great enough to compel acceptance and cause manager Branch Rickey to bring
him to Brooklyn. That first breach of the baseball color line occurred in 1947, when there was scant racial
integration of anything in America. Though hotly discussed, Rickey's action was widely applauded, and was
undoubtedly an important beginning of the social emancipations that grew over the next twenty years.
Robinson, an outstanding all-rounder of the game, was unmatched at that supremely appealing baseball
skill, stealing bases (2). "Watch him!" we rival fans would always cry to the pitcher whenever he was on
base. His abilities and strength of character attracted local fans and soon made him the preeminent
Dodger for baseball fans everywhere.
Ebbets Field's arched and pilastered exterior was built in 1913. The grandstands became more concentrated over the years, decreasing the size of the playing field along the foul lines. In 1957 the Dodgers
moved to Los Angeles at the same time that the New York Giants moved to San Francisco, and Ebbets
Field, Robinson's ramble, was torn down to become the site of Ebbets Field Apartments.

2

1

ADRENALIN AT THE OLD GARDEN. The Madison Square Garden of my youth was no longer in Madison Square and no longer sported a roof garden, but the promoter Tex Rickard's utilitarian third incarnation of the name was a financial success from its opening in November 1925. Rickard made it a renowned locus for boxing, professional hockey and basketball, while it continued to retain its earlier clientele of horse and dog shows, circuses, political conventions and rallies. Its closure and resettlement in 1968 would have caused little adverse comment but for the wanton destruction of Pennsylvania Station that its replacement helped make possible. Like other great arenas, though, the Eighth Avenue and 50th Street Garden had its powerfully emotional moments worth remembering, such as the depressing pro-Hitler rally by the German-American Bund on May 18, 1934 (1); and one of many victories by heavyweight Joe Louis in the city where the Brown Bomber's most devoted followers lived, the Louis-Conn fight of June 19, 1946 (2), when Louis KOed Billy Conn in the eighth round.

2

222

COLUMBIA COMMENCEMENT: STUDENT UPRISING. Columbia University happily continues to exist, but a memorable event that may always shadow it was the violent conflict between students on Morningside Heights and the New York police starting in February 1968. As a former Columbia student and faculty member, I followed the story from afar when ex-colleagues such as Ray Lifchez of the School of Architecture, who sympathized with the students, were beaten up. It began with a controversy surrounding Parks Commissioner Robert Moses's decision that Columbia could use part of Morningside Park as the site for a university gymnasium. Harlem residents resented the handover, which did not have popular support; activist Rap Brown's historic observation on the matter was "Burn, baby, burn." After years of negotiation with neighborhood representatives that did not bring about conditions of agreement, Columbia foolishly forced the issue by allowing the builders to start construction. That resulted in a sit-in by students in support of Harlem residents, some arrests, and, ten days later, the first big clash with police when members of the Students for a Democratic Society held a protest march and attempted to tear down the construction fence. Ill-timed sentiments in favor of wise authority were voiced by Diana Trilling and other pundits of the day. The ensuing violent campus demonstrations (including the occupation and trashing of the university president's office) captured world headlines that sparked off bigger conflicts involving students later in 1968 — at Berkeley, in Paris, and elsewhere. In New Haven, Yale's architecture and fine arts building was burned down. It all began in New York, at Columbia.

HAPPY EVENTS AND PARADES

New York has its own unique versions of common public events: the reception parade with ticker tape, the holiday parade with huge balloons, the social and fashion show in the street — which on Fifth Avenue is staged rather differently from the way it is carried out on Ocean Drive in Miami: with dignity (in my jaundiced recollection, anyhow). Enthusiastic display belongs in Times Square, of course.

1

THE EASTER PARADE, FIFTH AVENUE.   The New York custom of Easter Sunday fashion promenades along Fifth Avenue may have been largely usurped by publicity seekers and demonstrators, but for nearly a century Easter Parades were socially consequential and even commercially important. Begun by the 1870s, they evolved more or less naturally from the processionals and recessionals of smartly dressed churchgoers. By the 1880s dressmakers and milliners were coming to sketch outfits, and the press was sending photographers to lie in wait. Sketches were copied by garment makers on the Lower East Side, and photos were circulated to newspapers all over the country. By the 1930s both George M. Cohan and Irving Berlin had written songs about the annual event. (1) shows the impressive Fifth Avenue crowd outside St. Patrick's Cathedral on Easter 1954 in a view from the RCA Building.

Seen today, old photographs of the Easter Parade remain fascinating as detailed records of costume, body language and streetscape that are exactly identifiable by date, and for the occasional historical character who swings into view. The parades shown were in 1906 (2), 1908 (3) and 1911 (4). (5) is the result of a cameraman's ambush of two participants in the 1915 parade, Mr. and Mrs. Henry Clay Frick. Frick, a founder and director of Carnegie Steel and the U.S. Steel Corporation, had completed the building of his great house at 1 East 70th Street the previous year; when he died four years later he left the city his mansion and its collection of Renaissance paintings.

2

3

4

5

1

THE RECEPTION FOR LINDBERGH.

THE RECEPTION FOR LINDBERGH. Huge public acclaim often rewards triumphs of interconnectivity — for example, the opening of the transatlantic cable (1, lauding Cyrus G. Field on September 25, 1858, at New York City Hall) and the electrification of New York, celebrated in 1884 by parades of marchers in battery-lit headgear. The creators of the telegraph, the telephone and the Internet weren't honored by public jubilations, perhaps because their technological achievements weren't at first widely understood as having huge economic implications. But Charles Lindbergh's solo flight from New York to Paris on May 20, 1927, generated an enormous public response in recognition of his triumph of individual mobility. Earlier transatlantic fliers (on a shorter course via Labrador) had been a duo.

Lindbergh took off eastward from Roosevelt Field, Long Island, and reached Paris. Upon his return on June 13, New York staged a huge reception along Broadway (2). The air was filled with paper from reels used in the now obsolete stock market tickers, as well as toilet paper rolls and confetti from newspapers and office stationery; street cleaners later bore off 110 truckloads. "It beat a snowstorm all to pieces," said its recipient.

Lindbergh's reception wasn't the first of its kind in New York; there had been ticker-tape parades since the dedication of the Statue of Liberty in 1886. And it certainly hasn't been the last, as war heroes, astronauts and baseball teams often are now so received. But it was undoubtedly the most famous and memorable, and it may hold the record as the most litterful.

2

THE OPEN HYDRANT. The important New York street play of my childhood was the game of stickball amid parked cars, with a broomstick as bat and a pink rubber Spalding (or "spaldeen") ball. In the '60s, Frisbee tosses around parked cars were encountered more often. But through most of my lifetime, kids on hot tenement streets with little access to recreational facilities would open the street hydrants for instant soakings. Using a monkey wrench or a five-sided hydrant key hustled from the local firehouse, they made the fountain gush until firemen or police closed in and turned it off. New York hydrants still have the same cast-iron form, but their water supply taps are now equipped with more obdurate fastenings.

1

MACY'S EVANESCENT BUBBLES.   Comforting a dying friend, my fellow visitor said, "Look at it this way. What will you be missing, a few Macy's Thanksgiving Parades?" That struck me as a more inspiring existential reassurance than any mention of the loved ones, political upheavals and new novels that would be missed. When I approach my own demise, it will be a consolation to think about letting go of Macy's Thanksgiving Day Parades. They mark the passage of years irrevocably but similarly, changing very gradually.

A New York institution, the first Macy's Thanksgiving Parades had live animals that proved troublesome, so they were replaced by helium-filled balloons. Nowadays the sponsored balloons cost $200,000 or more, are built by experts who work for the department store, and have a place in the parade guaranteed for three years. On Thanksgiving Eve the flat balloons are mustered and filled at designated

2   3   4

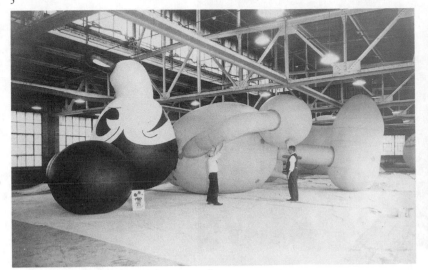

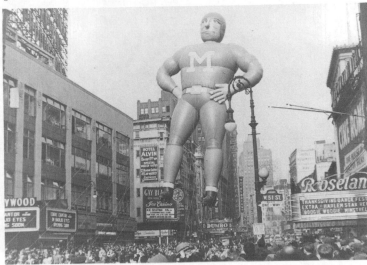

places in the West 70s between Central Park West and Columbus Avenue, and street encounters after that become surrealistic (1). The following day the inflated balloons are paraded down Central Park West and Broadway, interspersed with marching bands and celebrity floats.

Earlier balloons were less often sponsored, like the Eddie Cantor (2), the Mommy-I-want-one Felix the Cat (3) and the Tin Woodman of 1939 (4), its design clearly unrelated to the tin man in the filmed *Wizard of Oz* of the same year — and unrelated to the book, come to think of it, without the square patch on his chest that the Wizard cut to insert his silken heart.

The earlier Mickey Mouse (5) was built in Akron, Ohio, in 1935 by the Goodyear Tire and Rubber Company. Some of the early balloons were very large and not necessarily busting with charm, like 1941's monstrous 75-by-44-foot football player (6), bearing down on the Roseland Ballroom when it was at Broadway and 51st Street.

Contemporary Macy's balloons, like the Snoopy of 1999 (7), are built smaller — around 25 feet in the largest dimension — and are held down closer to the ground to reduce the chance of dangerous accidents. As thousands of viewers line the streets of New York and television shows them nationally, the tethered bubbles float by. We should be grateful that they evolve and change very slowly, so we can safely take leave of parades beyond us.

229

TIMES SQUARE, THE PLACE TO BE.   New York's great crowd events of the 19th century were held in Tompkins Square, Astor Place and Union Square. When the building of the subways and the current Grand Central Station, with its crosstown shuttle connection, made Broadway and 42nd Street the main urban transit interchange, Longacre Square took over the party. It was renamed Times Square when the *New York Times* built its office tower there.

As an urban plaza it isn't an elegant space: a long triangle connected to another long triangle (Duffy Square), with a ragged skyline and a single isolated crag (One Times Square, the former Times Tower),

rather like a ravine or a gulch for an Indian ambush. But what makes it attractive is precisely its unusual length (42nd to 47th Street is about 1,400 feet, or a quarter of a mile), width (tapering from about 265 feet at the ends to about 120 feet in the middle pinch, where Broadway and Seventh Avenue cross) and raggedness, plus its electric signs and centrality to entertainment. When completely turned over to pedestrian crowds, as it regularly is for New Year's Eve and public celebrations, it becomes a single vast space. Perhaps the eyes of the planet aren't always trained on Times Square, as local journalists proclaimed on January 1, 2000, but few other cities can concentrate more than half a million festive people at their center without stringing them out along a river or wrecking a park.

Some great Times Square moments have occurred in a space whose buildings are continually changing. On V-Day 1918 (1) the view is of a grandstand that may have been on 42nd Street. The 1919 view (2) looking south from 47th Street shows Times Square at the highly temporary pinnacle of its elegance, with Daniel Burnham's lost Rector Hotel of 1910 on the left in the middle distance, Cyrus Eidlitz's pre-alteration Times Tower in the center, and the lost Astor Hotel on the right. In the right foreground is the lost Gaiety Theater (see page 257), parallel to a vanished subway entrance building.

A refinement that greatly contributed to a sense of Times Square as the rightful civic agora was the moving news sign around Times Tower (3), elaborately done with thousands of incandescent bulbs before electronic moving signs became common. On May 8, 1945, the news of V-E Day arrived in a Times Square already prepared with a scale model of the Statue of Liberty (4, taken from the catwalk above the moving sign). The view the same evening from the top of the Times Tower shows the square spotlit with moving lights used by newsreel photographers (5), a sight unlikely to be seen ever again now that we have low-light photography. The Camel sign, lower right, blew large smoke rings across the square.

231

6

The most important New Year's Eve before the millennium was popularly deemed to be that of January 1, 1950 (6). The photo of the awesomely large celebratory Times Square crowd was taken from the marquee of the lost Paramount Theater and incidentally shows the vanished Loew's State Theater and the Bond sign (which wrapped around the space that previously had been the International Casino). Between the Bond figures — whose armatures had originally supported giant Pepsi-Cola bottles — the famous waterfall splashed noisily. It was the closest Times Square ever came to having a public fountain. And then there was the millennium New Year's Eve of January 1, 2000 (7).

7

232

DISASTERS

THE STANFORD WHITE KILLING.   The second and most elaborate of the four Madison Square Gardens was a great building — see pages 50–53 — but not lucky for its very talented architect, Stanford White. Still then sited at the northeast corner of Madison Square (where, coincidentally, the New York office of my publisher, Houghton Mifflin, is now located), that Garden was underfinanced, completed over budget, and almost immediately and continually lost money. But it was loved, especially by White, who lived in the multipurpose building for a while and enjoyed the pleasures of its popular roof garden with its dinner shows, at one of which he fatefully met the attractive performer Evelyn Nesbit Thaw, "the girl in the red velvet swing." In her most famous part she sat in one, swinging delightfully above the audience.

Her jealous husband, Harry K. Thaw, shot Stanford White in the roof garden on June 25, 1906, as shown in the sequence here superimposed on a photo following the police investigation. After a sensational trial that thoroughly defamed Thaw's victim and for years submerged the professional esteem he deserved, the killer was sent to a mental institution and later freed. So architect and building, both estimable, were lost with Madison Square Garden number two.

1

2

THE APOCALYPTIC TRIANGLE SHIRTWAIST FIRE & OTHERS.

The great significance of the Triangle Shirtwaist Company fire of March 25, 1911 (1), often called New York's worst fire tragedy, wasn't the casualty list, dreadful though it was, nor the gratifying results of fire safety acts and unionization of workers that followed. It was the arousal of altruistic public indignation on a scale unseen in New York since Lincoln spoke about slavery at Cooper Union.

Triangle Shirtwaist, not a worse-than-ordinary garment-making company of the era, occupied the top three of ten floors of the then-new Asch Building on Washington Place and Greene Street, just east of Washington Square. When the fire broke out, many of the 500 workers managed to escape, some helped over the rooftop by New York University students from the adjacent building. But the building's elevators then crashed, the overloaded single fire escape collapsed, and some exit doors were discovered to be locked. The fire engine ladders proved to be about thirty feet too short to reach the burning floors, and firemen's life nets were torn by multiple plunges. Within about fifteen minutes of the fire's start, 146 young women were killed, many by jumping to their deaths from the ninth-floor window ledges, as horrified bystanders would never forget. NYU now owns the building (2), renamed, which bears plaques declaring it a national historic landmark and a labor union monument. Doubtless it is very fire-safe now, but some of the building's users must feel haunted by its grim history.

An even worse fire tragedy occurred at a theater at 313 Washington Street in Brooklyn, when a backstage outbreak flared into the auditorium and caused an escape panic that killed 295 people. It seems not to be reckoned in the New York league with the Triangle Shirtwaist fire, since its date was December 5, 1876, and Brooklyn didn't become a New York borough until 1897. Another great fire in Brooklyn, at Coney Island in July 1932 (3), caused more devastation than death. It destroyed beachfront

3

amusements, rendered 5,000 people homeless and cut off thousands of bathers as the conflagration spread along the Boardwalk. A few years later the Coney Island Boardwalk was rebuilt by Parks Commissioner Robert Moses, who made certain that commercial amusements had no part of it.

In (4), a nighttime three-alarmer of July 1937, the ironic sign "Simply Add Boiling Water" on the side of the burning Ameko Kitchen Products building referred to the Hygrade All Beef Frankfurters advertised by the sign on the roof. For further irony, the building was on Water Street, Manhattan. The mayor of New York was then Fiorello La Guardia, a redoubtable fire attendee, as the cartoonist Alain Brustlein showed in a contemporary *New Yorker* (5).

4

5

235

1

GUNSELS AT THE HALF MOON & THE PARK SHERATON. Two New York hotels — one lost, one considerably altered — had murderous associations with celebrity gunmen, and the associations overlie the detached interest of the buildings.

The Half Moon Hotel (1), designed by George B. Post & Sons, opened in 1927 at Coney Island in the hope of turning the beach into a resort location rather than just a place for a day trip. Its Spanish Colonial style wouldn't have looked out of place in Santa Barbara or Boca Raton; perhaps Brooklyn was a bit of a stretch.

236

2

3

In about 1940 a distant cousin of mine, Abe "Kid Twist" Reles, turned fink against his former associates in Murder Incorporated, a kill-for-hire syndicate that included Martin "Bugsy" Goldstein and Harry "Pittsburgh" Strauss — both of whom Reles helped to indict and get executed — plus four others (2: at their first police interrogation, seated left to right are Strauss, Goldstein and Reles). As he prepared to testify against Lepke Buchalter and Albert Anastasia, Kid Twist was held in protective custody at the Half Moon Hotel by five police officers. While the cops were allegedly asleep on November 12, 1941, he perhaps leaned too far out a window. Sadly, he was found dead the next morning on the Half Moon kitchen roof below (3, showing covered body). It was said afterward that "the canary could sing, but he couldn't fly." (My parents kept the familial association from us children for many years.) Achieving no prestige apart from the notorious Reles incident, the Half Moon gave up on being a hotel. The navy took it over as a recuperation facility in 1943. When their lease ended it was sold to become a hospital in 1949, a geriatric center in 1954, and the site for housing units for the elderly in 1989, when it was demolished. Albert Anastasia's career continued fairly unhindered for 16 years after Kid Twist defenestrated. Then on October 25, 1957, he was shot to death by unknown assailants in the barbershop of the Park Sheraton Hotel on Seventh Avenue between 55th and 56th Streets (4, his body being removed), reminding some crime buffs — and *Great Gatsby* readers — of Arnold Rothstein's 1928 assassination at New York's Park Central Hotel. The Park Sheraton is currently known as the Omni Park Central Hotel. In the mid-1980s it was reclad in bronzy aluminum, like a large tacky reliquary for Anastasia. The barbershop is gone.

4

THE WEST SIDE HIGHWAY &
THE NORMANDIE.   My main memo-
ries of early childhood are that my father worked
somewhere called the Brooklyn Navy Yard, that
FDR's death inspired my friends and me to stand
at attention in the playground and salute him, and
that my uncle took the children on a drive down
the West Side Highway to see the *Normandie*
lying on its side. That day is my strongest memory — a conflux of the highway, the ship and early
childhood briefly coming together before they all
disappeared.

New Yorkers called all the highways along the
Hudson the West Side Highway, including the
earliest-built section from Rector to 72nd Street.
Demolished in the 1970s, it was originally known
as the Miller Elevated Highway, which Borough
President Julius Miller himself opened in 1930
(1). Meanwhile in a distant country, the Compagnie Générale Transatlantique's magnificent
83,000-ton liner *Normandie*, more than 1,000 feet
in length, was being completed at about the same
time, with art deco interiors and dining room
columns covered in Lalique glass.

The ship's fine fittings became of small concern in
wartime. When the United States entered the war
the *Normandie* was in port in New York and was
seized from the then-Vichy owners. Renamed the
Lafayette, it was to be refitted as a troopship.

The West Side Highway may have had primitive
ramps and safety standards, but it certainly had a
good view of the immediately adjacent midtown
Hudson piers where the greatest liners berthed,
such as the *Normandie* and the *Queen Mary* (2 —
the latter already painted camouflage gray). Tragically, on February 9, 1942, a welder's torch (or so it
was said) started a fire on the *Normandie/Lafayette*
that couldn't be stopped (3), and the ship capsized
in its Pier 88 berth. For many months it lay like an
exquisite corpse observable from the highway, as
my cousins and I saw from my uncle's car (4).

Later the *Normandie*'s superstructure was sal-
vaged. Still later, I've now learned, the hull was
raised and moved to the Brooklyn Navy Yard.
The U. S. Navy closed that in 1966.

238

1

A PLANE CRASHES INTO THE EMPIRE STATE BUILDING. On Saturday, July 28, 1945, seventeen days before the end of the war, a twin-engine army B-25 Mitchell bomber en route from Bedford, Massachusetts, to Newark got lost in fog and crashed into the 34th Street north elevation of the Empire State Building, 915 feet above street level. Burning wreckage fell below. The interiors on the 78th and 79th floors of the building were consumed by exploding gasoline, with flames that were seen up to the 86th-floor observatory (1).

One of the plane's engines tore clear through the building and landed on an adjacent rooftop on 33rd Street, where it destroyed a sculptor's penthouse studio. The other engine and part of the landing gear burst into an elevator shaft and fell to a subcellar 1,000 feet below, while burning fuel cascaded down stairways to the 75th floor. Fourteen people were killed, including clerical workers in the building and the bomber's crew of three, and twenty-six were injured.

More than a thousand people were in the Empire State Building at the time of the accident. About fifty

240

2

were in the 86th-floor observatory. They heard the tremendous crash and saw orange flames halfway around them outside, but the canned music never stopped playing. After the fire went out, the guards smashed some glass in the terrace doors for fresh air, then the visitors made their way down the fire-proof stairs. Mayor La Guardia, meanwhile, had directed his limousine to the building, taken an elevator to the 60th floor, and walked up the stairs from there.

The disaster left a ragged hole in the side of the Empire State Building and twisted some structural steel (2), but inspection by engineers, architects and the city's building department showed that the building's structural soundness had not been impaired. After all, a medium-sized plane flying at a couple of hundred miles per hour that hits a skyscraper in a single local spot is a puny force compared to an over-60-mile-per-hour gust of wind that hits the building's entire facade, which is sure to happen every few months. It takes the work of aliens using special effects, as in the 1996 film *Independence Day*, to guarantee a complete destruction job.

PLACES OF THE GREATS,
THE CELEBRITIES, THE RIFF RAFF

I hold the particular, and possibly gonzolingual, notion that places can be buildings but all buildings aren't places. For example, a garage, a warehouse or a long-distance telephone exchange probably wouldn't figure as a place in the sense I mean. What I mean by place here is a destination for eyes and ears and appetites.

Some of New York's best lost places were great buildings. Others were created because of fashion, fascination or low urges, and the accommodation was almost irrelevant.

1   2

THE OLD MET'S TOSCANINI, PUCCINI, CARUSO, CALLAS — AND AUDIENCE. The décor of the old Metropolitan Opera House badly needed refurbishment, and only its stagehands and artists can describe what they had to put up with backstage. But by the time the old Met was demolished, its dilapidated yet not obsolescent fabric had entirely fused with its audience's perceptual nerves and involuntary muscles.

Historically, what was lost was the opera house where the still young Arturo Toscanini (1) was artistic

242

3

director from 1908 to 1915, where Enrico Caruso (2) sang 626 performances, and where Giacomo Puccini's *La Fanciulla del West* had its world premiere in 1910 (3, a Met program listing all three), and his *Il Trittico* eight years later. The opera house that more than any other starred the thrilling divas Birgit Nilsson and Maria Callas (4), and where Marian Anderson broke the opera color bar in 1955. The opera house that made standees wait for hours on a narrow sidewalk where garment-rack pushers could commiserate with them (5), and where I was thrilled to have an alternate-Tuesday-night subscription.

4   5

THE LOST NIGHTCLUBS. True, all big cities have nightclubs. But the cities of America also had Prohibition, which generated the practical requirements of exclusivity, limited access and socially sanctioned wickedness that make good nightclubs really thrive. And only America had New York. Q.E.D., most of the greatest nightclubs were New York's former speakeasies, such as the Embassy Club (gone), the Central Park Casino (gone), the Stork Club (gone), El Morocco (pfffft).

While the crowds in all the nightclubs, as Cole Porter said, punished the parquet and the bars were packed with couples calling for more, vulture columnists such as Walter Winchell would sit with tarantula owners like Sherman Billingsley of the Stork Club (1) and discuss who should get a table in Siberia and who should be asked to leave. Meanwhile, celebrity photographers would let waiters turn the ashtrays so newspaper readers could see where Ernest Hemingway had spent the evening trying to maintain pleasantries with his wife, Martha Gellhorn (2), or they would just pop their bulbs at the dim banquette where what's-their-names, that extremely attractive foreign film couple (3), were ensconced (if the banquette in the photo had zebra stripes, it was El Morocco). The best nightclubs had clear attractions or rationales that could almost be reduced to tag lines. The Embassy Club on 57th Street near Sutton Place: "Dutch Schultz owns it." The Central Park Casino: "Jimmy Walker's hangout." (Those two were among the most elaborate and beautiful clubs. When Robert Moses became Parks Commissioner

6

7

under Mayor La Guardia, he showed his disapproval for Walker by peremptorily demolishing the Central Park Casino, which had a glittering interior by Joseph Urban — see page 59 — in a Calvert Vaux building that had been part of Central Park since the beginning.) The Stork Club officially opened in 1934 at 3 East 53rd Street (4, 5), but its attraction prior to Repeal in 1933 was being part of the cluster of speakeasies that existed in the 50s near Fifth. Fastidious café society customers and lefty film stars who disliked the restrictive admission policies of Billingsley and the viciousness of his regular guest Winchell headed for El Morocco (6), which might have been tagged "the supper club for liberals." (While "supper club" suggests a place for having a decent meal, that expectation was usually inaccurate. The term was a euphemism.)

Other important bygone nightclubs of the '30s and '40s were Billy Rose's Diamond Horseshoe (7), the Latin Quarter (8) and the 2,000-capacity International Casino on the east side of Broadway between 44th and 45th Streets (9), designed in 1937 by the movie palace architect Thomas Lamb with Donald Deskey, who had done Radio City Music Hall's interiors. The International was planned for big-band attractions; the topless gals came along in its later days, supplanted by the Bond sign with waterfall. The most memorable New York nightclub of the few I ever attended was the Versailles, where I took an impressed date after my high school prom in 1952. We loved the floor show, but even I could see that the joint was past its prime. The golden age of nightclubs was ending.

8

9

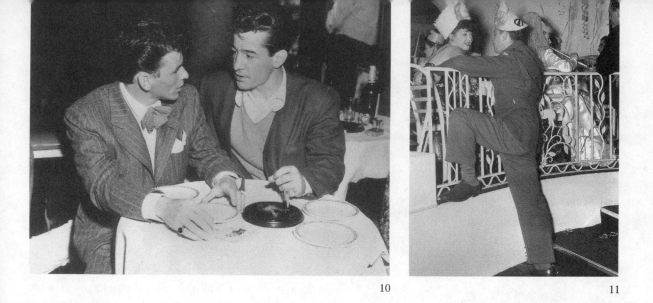

Perhaps the greatest New York nightclub, however, the Copacabana, at 10 East 60th Street, opened later and lasted longer than most (1940–1973, though a version has returned). Megastars such as Ella Fitzgerald, Nat King Cole and Frank Sinatra performed there and could be snapped at a table afterward with the likes of Rocky Graziano (10). Though the coconut-treed, rhumba-intimating Copa (12) was as expensive as any, it always harbored a refreshing proportion of proletarian customers, which made it the heaven of furlough destinations for World War II servicemen who fancied the chance to have a few words with Olga San Juan (11).

Before the speakeasies and since the Copa the nightclubs in New York have sometimes had other ideas of sexy entertainment, but they too have gone. (Lost Harlem clubs and jazz clubs are discussed on pages 248–50.) Studio 54, at 254 West 54th Street (1977–1988) was the greatest discothèque (13), and until the owners, Steve Rubell and Ian Schrager, were indicted for income tax evasion in 1979, they probably attracted as much publicity for their starry guests as Sherman Billingsley ever had. Studio 54 sanctioned its guests' semi-nudity and also immortalized a nasty new kind of restrictiveness, admission by street bouncer's selection (14). Downtown, the gay club and bathhouse Mineshaft (15) featured a Freely Box

13

14

for customers (16), and other raunchy events were notoriously staged. Meanwhile, at Plato's Retreat in the Ansonia on Broadway between 73rd and 74th Streets (17), the owner, Larry "King of Swing" Levenson, achieved the ultimate evening's entertainment: full sexual participation for all. Interior photographs are hard to come by, since customers were forbidden to bring cameras. However, the anteroom bulletin board advertised that videos could be arranged, and the duct-tape-mounted poster (a clever stylistic detail) suggested how to wear a towel on the premises (18). In the early '80s, Mineshaft and Plato's Retreat succumbed to AIDS concerns and were closed.

15

16

17

18

HARLEM IN ERMINE AND PEARLS.

Ironically, Harlem was most attractive to whiteys from the 1920s through the 1940s, a period of high segregation and discrimination. That was when Harlem culture began to flourish, and its music and dance were discovered by nightclubbers, critics and jazzers. There were hundreds of joints, most of the big ones owned by whites. Only white customers were allowed in some, such as Connie's Inn and the famous Cotton Club (1922–1937) at 142nd Street and Lenox Avenue (1, shown in 1925), owned by the white speakeasy proprietor Owney Madden. Duke Ellington started at the Cotton Club in 1927, Cab Calloway led the 1937 New Year's party (2), and other up-and-coming giants of American music performed there.

The big integrated venues would probably have had mostly black clientele if their prices had been lower. Smalls' Paradise Club (1925–1986), at 2294½ Seventh Avenue, featured Fats Waller, Willie "the Lion" Smith and Fletcher Henderson, among others, big stage shows, and stride piano. It also featured singing waiters on roller skates who served Chinese food. The Apollo Theater (opened in 1914, converted to a movie theater in 1975, and resumed live entertainment in 1983), at 253 West 125th Street (3), was no nightclub but a variety house. The Apollo booked the most famous Negro acts and ran talent contests at which the future greats Ella Fitzgerald and Sarah Vaughan emerged. The Savoy Ballroom (1926–1958), on Lenox Avenue between 140th and 141st Streets (4, in 1952), was the place to go to hear the big bands led by Ellington, Benny Goodman or Henderson dueling from stages at opposite sides of the dance floor. The ballroom held nearly 5,000, and it was where the Lindy Hop started — the customers all stompin' at the Savoy.

1

2

3

4

52ND STREET: SWING STREET.

"Good-Time Street," "Swing Street," "The Street That Never Slept," or just "The Street" — New York must be really rich to have thrown away a street like this. On 52nd between Fifth and Sixth Avenues, a roaring block of brownstones where clubs crowded each other, customers crowded in, and musicians worked, played, lived and wreaked radio broadcasts, you could walk through the history of jazz (1). The scene was crushed to smithereens in the early '50s when Lord & Taylor and MGM and Rockefeller Center developed new high-rise office buildings. And a second generation of big office buildings has since begun. Are we ahead or are we dead? Well, yesterday we had Billie Holiday, scat, blues and bebop spoken here; today, towering incommunicado. Ooblieadah!

The Swing Street phenomenon was sparked off in the 1920s by the historically capricious circumstance that Chicago started trying hard to enforce Prohibition and New York didn't, causing jazzers who lost jobs to move east. As a result, even before Duke Ellington really got going with big-band jazz at Harlem's Cotton Club, Fletcher Henderson was up and jumping at the Roseland Ballroom on Broadway and 51st Street (2 — the original Roseland was demolished in 1956), much abetted in performance and audience appreciation by Louis Armstrong, who left Chicago in 1924 for New York's recording and broadcasting studios and the Henderson band. Jazz in New York consolidated when Benny Goodman hired Henderson as arranger in 1934 after Henderson's band broke up, and Count Basie brought his orchestra to town in 1936. Taken with Ella Fitzgerald's emergence at the Savoy in Harlem in 1934 and Billie Holiday's singing dates downtown from 1939 on, the New Yorkers who noticed found that their town had noodled and jammed its way to becoming the national jazz powerhouse that New Orleans, Kansas City and even Chicago had never been. At the edge and sometimes the center of the action was Swing Street. Even if the jazzers weren't playing there, that's where they hung out.

52nd Street's real glories became obvious during World War II, when Coleman Hawkins came home from Europe, and afterward, with the emergence of Charlie Parker, Thelonious Monk (he graduated from my own Stuyvesant High School), and Dizzy Gillespie, who fashioned New York's jazz idiom, bop. Bop's happy home was Jimmy Ryan's (1), plus wherever Basie played — originally at 52nd Street's Famous Door. Smaller progressive groups played at the Downbeat, Kelly's Stable, the Hickory House, the Three Deuces and the Onyx. Swing Street's artistic apogee may have been 1949, when, with real estate demand already beginning to threaten the existing clubs, Birdland was opened at Broadway and 52nd Street by Charlie "Bird" Parker (3 — Parker shown on sax with Max Kaminsky, Lester Young, Hot Lips Page and Lennie Tristano). Sadly, the end was already nigh for the street, if not for the music. In 1953 the likes of heiress Doris Duke still hung out at Birdland to dig those gone sounds and get sent by the jive from the likes of Jay McNeely (4). But leases weren't being renewed, and New York jazz had started to devolve to the Village, Lincoln Center and even netherer regions.

250

3

4

42ND STREET, WHERE THE LIFE WAS. There's no call for scorn or resentment about West 42nd Street's change from its recent sleazy past (1) to the present strip of rebuilt theaters, media offices and family-directed retailing. One needn't invoke clichés like "sanitized" and "Disney-fied." After all, the street once had live theater and music publishing, so the not dissimilar rebirth should work. And a little cleanup probably won't prove fatal.

But those who insist that 42nd Street was all porno flicks and video shops, the criminal beat of perverts, druggies and prostitutes, regrettably overlook the vitality and fun that preceded that by thirty or fifty years, and undoubtedly continued to underlie the street's sleaze of later days. For one thing, 42nd Street used to be where the professional magic shops were. As a boy magician I spent Saturday mornings at a New York City–sponsored club run by Peter Pan the Magic Man (he was Shari Lewis's father and Lamb Chop's godfather). Afterward I would hit the 42nd Street shops with whatever money I had to buy magic books and tricks, as hundreds of others did. The stores were full of pro and semi-pro magicians on Saturdays, doing little performances for bystanders and telling us their stories.

Another great cultural asset of the street was the flea circus at Hubert's Museum, in the back of an arcade that hadn't yet become electronic (2). As I've learned, it was run by Herbert LeRoy Heckler, who inherited it from his father. Professor Heckler sat behind a table on a small platform and put his troupe through teeny circus acts, while we attendees, having paid about 50 cents for the performance, watched through magnifying glasses. The fleas danced, juggled, walked a tightrope, operated a carousel and ran a chariot race. Professor Heckler supplied them with the human blood on which they subsisted in exchange for the livelihood they supplied him. If we're getting a new 42nd Street now with improved commercial returns, it's a comfort that the economic deal will probably be no worse.

1

2

IT HAPPENED HERE

Many of the more expressive New York tocksteads — or, if we prefer wordiness, vanished place/moment convergences — flaunted the charms of the city's purposes and people, which have helped shape our own perceptions and sensibilities.

THE NEW YORK PIERS WITH MASTED SHIPS. When Berenice Abbott photographed *Changing New York* for the Federal Art Project in 1936, she waited days until the cargo schooner *Theoline* was on one of its rare visits to Pier 11, unloading potatoes from Massachusetts. She tried many exposures and lenses before producing her great image of the ship's diagonal rigging superimposed on buildings carefully aligned to be vertical and rectilinear (1). Pier 11, near Wall Street, was demolished two years later, and in 1942 the *Theoline* was wrecked in the West Indies. Abbott captured one of the last depictions of a masted ship serving the port of New York, the interference pattern of crossing lines from two eras and two ideas of structure becoming a graphic analysis of time and space. (It's poetically fitting that the same bit of waterfront has been proposed for the downtown Guggenheim Museum, which in Frank Gehry's design provides a new vision of contextual interference with prim old Wall Street.) The city's economic basis from the beginning was its seaport. As New York's mercantile strength and inland connections grew through the 19th century, the number of piers around the seaward end of Manhattan increased, the cargo tonnage multiplied, and the city population rose. Early photographs of the water's edge show the bristling activity in the way that only tall rigged ships can bristle. (2) is a photograph of 1859 from the steeple of Trinity Church, facing the Hudson piers and New Jersey. (3) was taken about 1870 of the South Street piers along the East River, and (4) is a panoramic view of 1882 or 1883 taken from the New York tower of the nearly complete Brooklyn Bridge. Beyond the buildings of the South Street brass and sail merchants, the highest buildings of New York appear on the skyline:

1

from left to right, the Cotton Exchange under construction (see page 101); Trinity Church; Bogardus's 217-foot shot tower of 1856 on Beekman Street (his second, at the time the tallest structure in the city apart from Trinity's steeple); the curved roof of the City Hall Post Office (pages 106–7). Below and to the right of the post office is the top part of Bogardus's Harper & Brothers building (page 167). In the foreground are the masts of the shallower-drawing packets and clippers that used the East River piers.

In our time the conveyance of goods has turned to bulk containers and consolidated depots, with distribution via interwoven transport reticulations. We expect networks to be endless grids rather than the plainly radiating webs of the past, which indicated purpose and direction. Even our ships are now hulls without visually apparent means of propulsion. A great port looked different when all the mechanics of distribution and transportation were visible.

THE VIEW FROM ELLIS ISLAND. After the U.S. Immigration and Naturalization Service moved to Manhattan in the 1950s, Ellis Island was abandoned; it was not clear how the surplus property could be used. In the 1960s President Johnson declared it a national monument, but Congress declined to appropriate any funds. At the time I thought the site should be allowed to have a living population and a useful purpose, such as a new university. At last, in 1984, a Reagan-appointed commission set up a private foundation to raise funds for the island's restoration as a historic site. Ellis Island, much of it still unrestored, has begun to be transformed into a museum of immigration and a sort of national shrine. That use seems justifiable and correct.

Australia also had a landing station and processing center for immigrants, but theirs was for subjects involuntarily bound for thralldom and servitude. Ellis Island was for people freely choosing a new motherland and the pursuit of happiness. In the mass immigration years between 1892 and 1924, 16 million people (including my four grandparents) came through Ellis Island — 71 percent of all the contemporaneous immigrants to the United States. And a large proportion of them remained in or near New York.

The oddly rectilinear shape of the island seen in aerial photos was the result of landfill, which built the original 3-acre island to the more practical size of 27.5 acres, as required by the burgeoning immigrant center. From that odd geometrical island on the edge of the former Oyster Banks in the Upper Bay, new arrivals could gaze across four and a half miles of water at the wondrous skyline of the city and consider its messages. The prospect must have raised wild surmise. Among its marvels were the 1913 Woolworth Building, the 1908 Singer Tower, the 1915 Equitable Building and, in the distance in middle Manhattan, the 1909 Metropolitan Life Tower, all the tallest buildings in the world.

254

1

2

3

THE OLD SHOPS.
My grandparents Sophie and Hyman Nachimowsky ran a typical New York neighborhood candy store at 260 Audubon Avenue in Manhattan, near 178th Street (1). My greatest adventure as a small child in about 1940 was taking a Sunday trolley trip with my mother from the East Bronx to Washington Heights to see my grandparents. The slow, somewhat sickening gait of the trolleys (and it was a gait, almost as if horses were still connected) took more than an hour. Mother taught me to read by having me work out the pronunciation of the names of Chinese restaurants along the route.

At the candy store there never seemed to be many customers. Grandma would make me a chocolate ice cream soda. I would hang out at the shop with my mother and sister (2 — I'm past the learning-to-read age), sometimes helping out by making an egg cream or locating a new tin box of straight pretzels. My grandparents gave up the store when the block was demolished to make room for part of "Heartbreak Highway," the resident-dispossessing link to the George Washington Bridge for Robert Moses's Cross-Bronx Expressway.

Another old shop, or shall we say joint, was run by Nathan, my paternal grandfather: Silver's Tavern, probably at 61 Broome Street. No photographs of it seem to exist. I suspect that Grandpa and my aunt Bess (3) are pictured standing in the street just outside it. When my father worked behind the bar in the early '30s, the booze was kept in open jars. He was told to dash the contents against the wall in case of a raid (if it was poured into the sink, the trap could be opened for evidence). But he said the saloon was never raided because the local politicos drank there. Grandma Esther made oyster stew for customers without ever tasting it because it wasn't kosher. I noticed that my father had quite a good opinion of it.

Grandpa sold Silver's Tavern to a cousin sometime before Repeal. If it was on Broome Street, had Moses's Lower Manhattan Expressway been built, it too would have been demolished. At any rate it isn't there now.

255

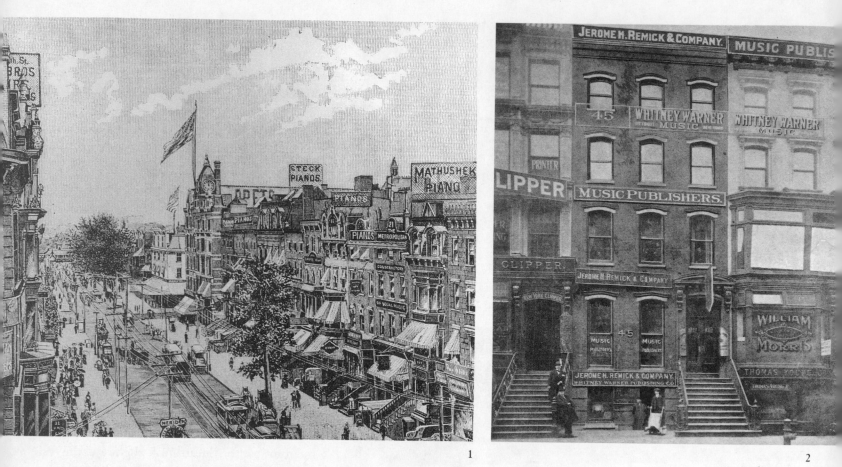

1

2

TIN PAN ALLEY, A MOVEABLE FEAST.　　Tin Pan Alley was (and sometimes still is) a conceptual or virtual place, not a real site or address. Like many New York clusterings, it started here, moved to there and ended up somewhere else. Its genesis lay with the song publishers, the piano companies that also ran retail music shops, and the piano-playing song pluggers who mercilessly flogged songs to whoever might be listening — in return for very little money other than possible publication deals for their own songs (the work was better than being a singing waiter, the other popular option, which Irving Berlin, among others, tried). The music publishing industry really started to focus on the possibilities of the business in 1892, when the sheet music for that scarcely great song "After the Ball" sold more than 5 million copies. At that point the whole congregation was clustered around the piano companies' music shops on 14th Street west of Broadway (1).

When the big music publisher M. Witmark and Sons decided to move, the next tribal location became 28th Street between Broadway and Sixth Avenue. In the photo (2) of part of that street in 1914, the signboards of several other music publishers and the William Morris Agency can be seen.

That favored location lasted less than ten years. The rise of the musical theater's new songwriters in the late teens and '20s encouraged another change of neighborhood, and soon some Tin Pan Alleycats were beginning to move to the new theater center on West 42nd Street. But that didn't remain the hot music district for long either. In the early 1930s there was a concerted move of publishers and agents to the Brill Building on Broadway and 49th Street, probably because the movie palaces that played live musical performances and bought sheet music had spread up Broadway, as had some new large auditorium theaters.

The Tin Pan Alley buildings didn't look like much, and weren't. They were mere addresses for something invisible, the encouragement and commercialization of American popular music.

256

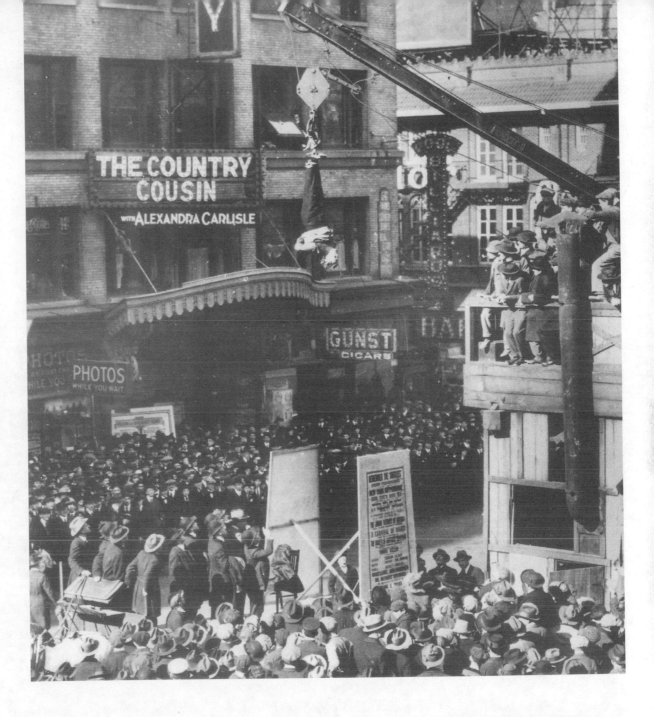

HOUDINI ON BROADWAY. Harry Houdini arrived in New York at the age of twelve with the name Ehrich Weiss. By 1917, when this photograph was taken, he was a world-famous escapologist (and, in the 1940s, a role model for a boy magician). Later he became an implacable exposer of spiritualist fakers (which I also quite approved of).

There are many marvelous photos showing Houdini in chains, in tanks of water, and being hauled out of rivers. This is the best: hanging from a crane upside down in a straitjacket at the southwest corner of Broadway and 46th Street, before he effected his invariably rapid escape for the adoring crowd. Investigation reveals that *The Country Cousin* was playing at the Gaiety Theater, and that gives us the address (the site is visible in full in 2, page 230) and the date. The Gaiety was built in 1908 by the distinguished theater architects Henry Herts and Hugh Tallant. In 1932 it became a burlesque house, and in 1943 it was turned into a movie theater and renamed the Victoria. It was demolished in 1982. Houdini died in 1926 after being caught off guard by a punch to the abdomen to test his musculature.

HOOVERVILLE, CENTRAL PARK. Of the twenty-odd Hoovervilles that sprang up around New York during the Depression (1), the most impudent and influential was the shantytown in Central Park. It was built from ad hoc materials on a site not unreasonably or inconsiderately chosen, the barren drained bed of the Lower Reservoir that is now the park's Great Lawn. But because it lacked obscuring landscaping and thus was plainly in view from Fifth Avenue and the Metropolitan Museum of Art (2), complaints about it led to arrests in July 1931 (3).

The disquieting Hoovervilles were celebrated in song and story, notably by the films *Hallelujah I'm a Bum*, *The Grapes of Wrath*, *Sullivan's Travels* and latterly (with a Hooverville scene set specifically in Central Park) the musical *Annie*, in which the denizens sing, "We'd like to thank you, Herbert Hoover, / You made us what we are today."

1

2

3

MAYOR LA GUARDIA'S CITY.

Fiorello La Guardia was elected mayor in 1933, the year after he lost his congressional seat in the Roosevelt landslide. That he was a Republican didn't prevent his becoming a great friend of FDR, who likewise admired the Little Flower (3). The mayor's ideas about uniting fragmented political responsibilities, his defense of labor and his proposals for civic improvements influenced the New Deal, and at the end of his mayoral career he accepted a presidential nomination to become the first head of the U.N. Relief and Rehabilitation Administration.

It's difficult to choose the best tockstead for La Guardia among the many colorful possibilities. Perhaps not racing to fires, sledgehammering slot machines, smoking large cigars, reading the funnies over WNYC during the 1945 newspaper strike or throwing out opening-day baseballs — even Mayor John Lindsay could have done that stuff. La Guardia's modernization of municipal government and his obtaining of huge federal grants for New York were notable, but scarcely reducible to a tockstead-bite. Everything he did was determined, honest and friendly. He was a model democratic leader, one might say, if "democratic" was a word people could parse to understand what a great politician should be.

I suppose La Guardia's ability and optimism are best represented by two images that show a couple of his New York achievements, even if they weren't precisely personal moments: his glowing attendance at the opening of the 1939 World's Fair with Henry and Edsel Ford, Al Smith and Grover Whalen (1); and a view of the airport he nagged the federal government for, in its early days as New York Municipal Airport (2). Of course, La Guardia Airport (now vastly extended) soon became a rare case of a public work deservedly renamed in honor of the sitting politician who had achieved it.

2

1

3

ILLUSTRATIONS AND SOURCES.

A description of the illustration is followed by the date it was made, when obtainable; and the maker (the photographer unless otherwise indicated), when known. The last listing is the source.
Midtown compass directions are conventionalized, with avenues considered to be running north-south.

THE URBAN SCENE AND PUBLIC PLACES.   22

23   *The Plaza, 59th Street and Fifth Avenue, showing old Plaza Hotel (right). Looking south.*
New York Public Library.

24(1)   *Central Park South, looking east to Hotel Netherland on Fifth Avenue.* Ca. 1925. Private
collection.

24(2)   *The Plaza, showing Pulitzer fountain, "Marble Row" (left) and Cornelius Vanderbilt II house
(right). Looking southeast.* Ca. 1925. Wurts Brothers.

25(3)   *The Plaza, showing Pulitzer fountain and Cornelius Vanderbilt II house (center). Looking
south.* Before 1927. Private collection.

25(4)   *The Plaza, showing Savoy-Plaza Hotel (left) and Bergdorf Goodman store (right). Looking
southeast.* 1931. Wurts Brothers.

26(1)   *Washington Inaugural Centennial wooden arch, Fifth Avenue and Washington Square North.
Looking northeast.* 1889. Museum of the City of New York.

26(2)   *Columbus Quatercentenary Arch, Fifth Avenue and 58th Street. Looking north from 57th Street.*
1892. New-York Historical Society.

27(3)   *Dewey Arch, Fifth Avenue between 23rd and 24th Streets, showing Fifth Avenue Hotel (left),
and intersection of streets with Broadway (diagonal trolley tracks). Looking north.* 1899.
A. Wittemann. New-York Historical Society.

28(1)   *Grand Central Terminal, 1871 building, 42nd Street at end of Fourth Avenue. Looking northwest.* H. N. Tiemann. Private collection.

28(2)   *Grand Central Terminal, 1899 building, 42nd Street at end of Fourth Avenue. Looking northwest.* Courtesy Columbia University School of Architecture.

29(1)   *Park Avenue, showing New York Central building. Looking south.* Wurts Brothers.

30(2)   *Park Avenue vehicle ramp at Grand Central Terminal, above Vanderbilt Avenue. Looking
south.* Courtesy Columbia University School of Architecture.

31(3)   *Grand Central Terminal, showing Park Avenue vehicle ramp. Looking northeast.* Wurts
Brothers.

31(4)   *Grand Central Terminal entablature sculpture, and roof of New York Central building. Looking
north.* Courtesy Avery Architectural Library.

33(1)   *Pennsylvania Station, Seventh Avenue between 31st and 33rd Streets. Looking northwest.*
Courtesy Pennsylvania Railroad Company.

34(2)   *Pennsylvania Station Train Concourse roof, aerial view looking northwest. Construction progress
photo.* 1910. Courtesy Avery Architectural Library.

35(3)   *Pennsylvania Station. Interior of Train Concourse roof.* 1963. Nathan Silver.

35(4)   *Pennsylvania Station. Interior of Train Concourse, showing track and platform levels. Looking
northeast. Construction progress photo.* 1910. Courtesy Avery Architectural Library.

36(5)   *Pennsylvania Station. Interior of General Waiting Room. Looking north.* Courtesy Pennsylvania Railroad Company.

36(6)   *Pennsylvania Station. South Carriage Driveway, looking west.* Courtesy Avery Architectural
Library.

37(7)	*Pennsylvania Station. Interior showing Train Concourse, looking northwest.* Courtesy Avery Architectural Library.
38(8)	*Pennsylvania Station. Interior of General Waiting Room, looking northwest during demolition.* 1963. Nathan Silver.
38(9)	*Pennsylvania Station. North Carriage Driveway, looking west during demolition.* 1963. Nathan Silver.
39(1)	*Central Park, between 102nd and 103rd Streets.* New York Public Library.
40(2)	*Central Park bandstand.* Courtesy Ware Memorial Library, Columbia University School of Architecture.
41(3)	*Central Park.* Byron. Museum of the City of New York.
42(1)	*Lower Fifth Avenue from atop Washington Arch, showing Brevoort Hotel (white building on right). Looking north.* Wurts Brothers.
43(2)	*Park Avenue between 50th and 51st Streets, showing Sheraton East Hotel (right, beyond St. Bartholomew's Church). Looking north.* Byron. New-York Historical Society.

PRIVATE GATHERING PLACES. *44*

45	*The Panhellenic. Interior of tower lounge. Northeast corner First Avenue and 49th Street.* Private collection.
46	*Broadway Tabernacle interior. Broadway between Worth Street and Catherine Lane.* Engraving from *Frank Leslie's Illustrated Newspaper*, March 15, 1856. Author's collection.
47	*Niblo's Garden interior, northeast corner Broadway and Prince Street.* Ca. 1845. Watercolor by B. J. Harrison. Museum of the City of New York.
48	*German Winter Garden interior. 45 Bowery.* 1856. Watercolor by Fritz Meyer. Museum of the City of New York.
49	*Atlantic Garden interior. 50 Bowery between Bayard and Canal Streets.* Engraving from *Harper's Magazine*, April, 1871. New York Public Library.
50(1)	*Great Roman Hippodrome, between Madison and Fourth Avenues, 26th and 27th Streets, showing Leonard Jerome house (right). Looking north up Madison Avenue.* Courtesy Columbia University School of Architecture.
51(2)	*Madison Square Garden, between Madison and Fourth Avenues, 26th and 27th Streets, showing Leonard Jerome house (right). Looking northeast from Madison Square Park.* New-York Historical Society.
52(3)	*Madison Square Garden interior, showing cattle show.* 1895. Byron. Museum of the City of New York.
53(4)	*Madison Square Garden, looking southeast down Madison Avenue.* 1895. New-York Historical Society.
54(1)	*Tammany Hall interior. North side of 14th Street, between Third Avenue and Irving Place.* Color lithograph, 1888. Courtesy Cooper Union Museum Library.
55(2)	*Tammany Hall, showing Academy of Music (left). Looking northwest.* 1881? New-York Historical Society.
56(1)	*Broadmoor Restaurant interior. East 41st Street.* Ca. 1930. Samuel H. Gottscho.
56(2)	*Pennsylvania Station Dining Room interior.* Courtesy Avery Architectural Library.
57(3)	*Claremont Inn, Riverside Drive near 125th Street. Aerial view looking northwest.* Wurts Brothers.
58(4)	*Delmonico's, northeast corner Fifth Avenue and 44th Street. Looking northeast.* Wurts Brothers. Museum of the City of New York.
59(5)	*Central Park Casino interior, the Black and Gold Room. Central Park.* 1933. New York Public Library.
60(6)	*Crillon Restaurant, 116 East 48th Street.* Private collection.
61	*Canfield's Gambling House, interior showing Gaming Room. 5 East 44th Street.* Private collection.
62(1)	*Waldorf Hotel, interior of Turkish Salon. Northwest corner of Fifth Avenue and 33rd Street.* Private collection.
62(2)	*Waldorf-Astoria Hotel, interior of Peacock Alley. Between Fifth and Sixth Avenues, 33rd and 34th Streets.* Private collection.
63(3)	*Waldorf-Astoria Hotel. Looking southwest.* Ca. 1919. New-York Historical Society.

64(4) *Manhattan Beach Hotel, Coney Island, Brooklyn. Looking northeast?* Stereoscope photograph. New-York Historical Society.

65(5) *Grand View Hotel, Fort Hamilton, Brooklyn.* 1888. New-York Historical Society.

66(6) *Park Avenue Hotel, Park Avenue between 32nd and 33rd Streets. Looking southwest.* From *Select New York,* published by Adolph Wittemann, 1889–90. Author's collection.

67(7) *Murray Hill Hotel, Park Avenue between 40th and 41st Streets. Detail.* Ca. 1937. Berenice Abbott. Museum of the City of New York.

68(8) *Astor House, Broadway between Vesey and Barclay Streets. Looking west.* Courtesy Columbia University School of Architecture.

68(9) *Fifth Avenue Hotel, Fifth Avenue between 23rd and 24th Streets. Looking northwest.* Ca. 1885. Courtesy Columbia University School of Architecture.

69(10) *Savoy Hotel, showing Bolkenhayn Apartments (right). East side of Fifth Avenue, between 58th and 59th Streets. Looking east.* Wurts Brothers. New York Public Library.

69(11) *Ritz-Carlton Hotel, Madison Avenue and 46th Street. Looking west.* Courtesy Columbia University School of Architecture.

70(12) *Ritz-Carlton Hotel interior.* Byron. Museum of the City of New York.

70(13) *Ritz-Carlton Hotel interior.* Byron. Museum of the City of New York.

71(14) *Buckingham Hotel, Fifth Avenue between 49th and 50th Streets. Looking northeast.* 1913. New-York Historical Society.

72(1) *Center Theater, Rockefeller Center, Men's Smoking Room interior. Sixth Avenue between 48th and 49th Streets.* Private collection.

73(2) *Center Theater auditorium interior.* 1932. Samuel H. Gottscho.

74(3) *Park Theater interior. Park Row.* Woodcut by Lansing, 1805. New-York Historical Society.

75(4) *Chatham Garden Theater interior. Chatham Street between Duane and Pearl Streets.* Lithograph from drawing by A. J. Davis. New-York Historical Society.

76(5) *Broadway Athenaeum, east side of Broadway at Waverly Place. Looking southeast.* 1874. New-York Historical Society.

77(6) *The Bowery (Thalia) Theater, 46 Bowery. Looking north.* 1914. New York Public Library.

78(7) *Academy of Music, 14th Street between Third Avenue and Irving Place. Looking northeast.* New-York Historical Society.

79(8) *Academy of Music auditorium interior.* Engraving from *Ballou's Pictorial Drawing-Room Companion,* ca. 1854. Author's collection.

80(9) *Pike's (Grand) Opera House, northwest corner of Eighth Avenue and 23rd Street. Looking northwest?* 1937. Berenice Abbott. Museum of the City of New York.

80(10) *Pike's (Grand) Opera House. Detail.* 1936. Berenice Abbott. Museum of the City of New York.

81(11) *Théâtre Français (Civic Repertory), 14th Street west of Sixth Avenue.* 1936. Berenice Abbott. Museum of the City of New York.

82(12) *The New Theater, Central Park West and 62nd Street. Looking southwest.* 1909. Frances B. Johnson.• Courtesy Columbia University School of Architecture.

82(13) *The New Theater. Interior of Main Vestibule.* 1909. Frances B. Johnson. New York Public Library.

83(14) *The New Theater. Interior of auditorium.* 1909. Frances B. Johnson. New York Public Library.

84(15) *Loew's 72nd Street. South side of 72nd Street west of Third Avenue. Lobby interior.* Courtesy Loew's Theatres.

84(16) *Loew's 72nd Street. Mezzanine Promenade interior.* Courtesy Loew's Theatres.

85(17) *Loew's 72nd Street. Auditorium interior.* Courtesy Loew's Theatres.

86(18) *Casino Theater, southeast corner of Broadway and 39th Street. Looking southeast.* From *Select New York,* published by Adolph Wittemann, 1889–90. Author's collection.

86(19) *Fulton Theater.* Courtesy Columbia University School of Architecture.

87(20) *Earl Carroll Theater. Lobby interior.* New York Public Library.

CIVIC ARCHITECTURE.   88

89 *The Croton Reservoir, Fifth Avenue from 40th to 42nd Streets. Looking southwest and showing the Hotel Bristol (right, demolished 1929).* Ca. 1893. H. N. Tiemann. Private collection.

90	*Federal Hall, northeast corner Wall and Nassau Streets. Looking northwest.* Engraving ca. 1792, by Cornelius Tiebout. Museum of the City of New York.
91	*Government House, Bowling Green and State Street.* Aquatint by William Rollinson. Private collection.
92(1)	*Fire Tower, 33rd (43rd?) Street near Ninth Avenue.* Engraving from *Illustrated News*, January 22, 1853. Author's collection.
92(2)	*Shot Tower. Section.* Engraving. Museum of the City of New York.
93(3)	*Shot Tower. 63–65 Centre Street.* H. N. Tiemann. Private collection.
94	*St. Luke's Hospital, west side of Fifth Avenue at 54th Street. Looking northwest.* H. N. Tiemann. Private collection.
95	*Tompkins Market and Armory, east side of Bowery between 6th and 7th Streets. Looking northeast.* 1911. Courtesy of the Cooper Union Museum.
96(1)	*Castle Garden interior: "First Appearance of Jenny Lind in America." Battery Park.* 1850. Color lithograph published by N. Currier. New-York Historical Society.
97(2)	*Castle Garden: "Interior of Castle Garden at the time of Max Maretzek's benefit."* Engraving, 1852. New York Public Library.
97(3)	*Castle Garden. Looking west.* Courtesy Columbia University School of Architecture.
98(1)	*U.S. Assay Office, 30 Wall Street, showing Sub-Treasury building (left). Looking northeast.* Courtesy Columbia University School of Architecture.
98(2)	*U.S. Assay Office showing Sub-Treasury building (left). Looking northwest.* Courtesy Columbia University School of Architecture.
99(1)	*Columbia College, 49th Street and Madison Avenue. Looking northeast.* From *Select New York*, published by Adolph Wittemann, 1889–90. Author's collection.
99(2)	*Columbia College, 50th Street and Madison Avenue. Looking southeast.* Courtesy Columbia University School of Architecture.
100	*Firehouse, Park Avenue and 135th Street. Looking northeast.* 1937. Berenice Abbott. Museum of the City of New York.
101	*Cotton Exchange, William and Beaver Streets.* Courtesy Columbia University School of Architecture.
102(1)	*Produce Exchange, Bowling Green and Beaver Street, showing "Steamship Row" (right). Looking east.* Courtesy Columbia University School of Architecture.
103(2)	*Produce Exchange, showing sculpture by D. C. French on Custom House (right). Looking east.* Ca. 1936. Berenice Abbott. Museum of the City of New York.
103(3)	*Produce Exchange. Main hall interior.* From *Select New York*, published by Adolph Wittemann, 1889–90. Author's collection.
104(1)	*Jefferson Market Prison, southeast corner of Greenwich Avenue and 10th Street. Looking east.* 1900. Courtesy Margot Gayle.
105(2)	*First Tombs Prison, Leonard and Centre Streets.* Private collection.
105(3)	*Second Tombs Prison, Center, Leonard, Elm and White Streets.* Courtesy Columbia University School of Architecture.
106(1)	*New York Post Office at City Hall, between Broadway, Park Row, and Park Place. Looking north.* Wurts Brothers. New York Public Library.
106(2)	*New York Post Office at City Hall. Detail.* Ca. 1937. Berenice Abbott. Museum of the City of New York.
107(3)	*New York Post Office at City Hall, showing Singer Tower (left in distance), Woolworth Building (tallest building), City Hall (right foreground). Aerial view looking southwest.* Ewing Galloway.
108(4)	*New York Post Office at City Hall. Looking south down Broadway.* 1908. Wurts Brothers. New York Public Library.
109	*Museum of Modern Art, 11 West 53rd Street. Looking northwest.* Wurts Brothers.

GREAT HOUSES.	110	
111		*Cornelius Vanderbilt II house, Fifth Avenue and 58th Street end. Looking west and showing the second Plaza Hotel (right).* Byron. Museum of the City of New York.
112		*Apthorpe house, near 91st Street and Columbus Avenue.* Courtesy Ware Memorial Library, Columbia University School of Architecture.

THE NEW YORK ROW HOUSE.   128

APARTMENT HOUSES.   138

142   *Studio Building, 51–55 West 10th Street. Looking northeast.* Ca. 1936. Berenice Abbott. Museum of the City of New York.

143   *The Knickerbocker Apartments. Fifth Avenue and 28th Street.* New York Public Library.

CHURCHES.   *144*

144(1)   *(1) Jones Chapel, East 64th Street. (2) Mount Washington Church, Broadway and Dyckman*
145(2)   *Street.* Latter by Wurts Brothers. Both from a private collection.

146   *Brick Presbyterian Church, northeast corner of Beekman and Nassau Streets.* Engraving from *Frank Leslie's Illustrated Newspaper*, May 10, 1856. Author's collection.

147   *Middle Dutch Church, Lafayette Place (Street).* Engraving made by Whitney Jocelyn. New York Public Library.

148(1)   *Madison Square Presbyterian Church, southeast corner of Madison Avenue and 24th Street.* Drawing of 24th Street elevation, probably by office of McKim, Mead and White. Courtesy Avery Architectural Library.

148(2)   *Madison Square Presbyterian Church. Looking northeast.* Courtesy Avery Architectural Library.

149   *Church of the Holy Trinity (Episcopalian), northeast corner of Madison Avenue and 42nd Street. Looking northeast.* H. N. Tiemann. Private collection.

150   *Temple Emanu-El, northeast corner of Fifth Avenue and 42nd Street. Looking east.* 1924. Byron. Courtesy of Cushman & Wakefield, Inc.

151(1)   *St. John's Chapel (Episcopalian), Varick Street between Laight and Beach Streets. Looking north.* Private collection.

152(?)   *St. John's Chapel. Interior, showing Choir and Gallery.* Private collection.

153(3)   *St. John's and St. John's Park. Looking southeast.* New-York Historical Society.

153(4)   *St. John's, showing Hudson River Railroad Freight Depot (right). Looking southeast.* Wurts Brothers. Private collection.

MOVEMENT.   *154*

155   *The Bronx-Whitestone Bridge, between the Bronx and Queens.* Philip D. Gendreau.

156   *1871 Grand Central train shed, Fourth (Park) Avenue. Looking north.* New-York Historical Society.

157   *Open top double-decker bus, on Fifth Avenue.* Ewing Galloway.

158   *Terminal of Hoboken Ferry, West Street at 23rd Street. Looking west.* 1935. Berenice Abbott Museum of the City of New York.

159   *Subway entrance kiosk, 50th Street east of Broadway. Looking west.* 1963. Nathan Silver.

COMMERCE.   *160*

161   *French Line pier, West Street between Horatio and Jane Streets? Looking east?* Stereoscope photograph. New-York Historical Society.

162   *Western Union building. Broadway and Dey Streets. Looking northwest?* From *Select New York*, published by Adolph Wittemann, 1889–90. Author's collection.

163   *Bank of America building, northwest corner of Wall and William Streets. Looking northwest.* New York Public Library.

164   *Worth Street, from Church Street to Broadway. Looking southwest.* From *The New Metropolis*, by E. Idell Zeisloft, 1899. Author's collection.

165   *The German Savings Bank building, southeast corner of Fourth Avenue and 14th Street. Looking southeast.* New York Public Library.

166   *Eccentric Mill Works, Centre and Duane Streets.* 1849 Lithograph by Ackerman. Museum of the City of New York.

167   *Harper & Brothers building, 331 Pearl Street, Franklin Square. Looking southwest.* Ca. 1870. Museum of the City of New York.

168(1)   *A. T. Stewart (old Wanamaker) store, between Broadway and Fourth Avenue, 9th and 10th Streets. Looking northeast?* Stereoscope photograph. New-York Historical Society.

168(2)   *A. T. Stewart (old Wanamaker) store. Looking northwest.* From *Select New York*, published by Adolph Wittemann, 1889–90. Author's collection.

169(1)   *New York Herald building, between Broadway and Sixth Avenue, 35th and 36th Streets. Looking northwest.* 1895. New-York Historical Society.

169(2)   *New York Herald building, looking north.* 1900? New-York Historical Society.

170(1)   *Times Tower, between Seventh Avenue and Broadway, 42nd and 43rd Streets. Looking northwest.* Private collection.

171(2)   *Times Tower. Looking south.* Picture postcard, showing scene on New Year's Eve. New-York Historical Society.

171(3)   *Times Tower. Looking northeast, during removal of exterior walls.* 1963. Nathan Silver.

172   *New York Telephone Company building, interior of Booth Room. 140 West Street.* Sigurd Fischer.

173   *Chrysler Building, interior of Observation Lounge. Between Lexington and Third Avenues, 42nd and 43rd Streets.* Private collection.

174   *Black, Starr & Frost building, southwest corner of Fifth Avenue and 48th Street. Looking southwest.* Ca. 1912. New-York Historical Society

175   *Lord & Taylor building, southwest (corner) of Broadway and 20th Street. Lookings outhwest.* Wurts Brothers. New York Public Library.

176(1)   *Merchants Exchange, 55 Wall Street. Looking south.* 1837 lithograph by William C. Kramp after drawing by Isaiah Rogers. Courtesy First National City Bank.

176(2)   *55 Wall Street, interior showing pneumatic system.* Courtesy First National City Bank.

177(3)   *55 Wall Street, interior of main banking floor.* Courtesy First National City Bank.

178(1)   *Food market, Broadway and 95th Street.* Wurts Brothers. New York Public Library.

178(2)   *Windsor Arcade, east side of Fifth Avenue between 46th and 47th Streets. Looking northeast.* Wurts Brothers. New York Public Library.

179(3)   *Commercial building, west side of Madison Avenue between 59th and 60th Streets. Looking southwest.* Private collection.

179(4)   *Loft candy store, Broadway and 90th Street.* Ca. 1930. Private collection.

PUBLIC AMUSEMENTS.   *180*

181   *"Elephantine Colossus," Coney Island, Brooklyn.* Advertising card. New-York Historical Society.

182(1)   *Crystal Palace, east side of Sixth Avenue between 40th and 42nd Streets. Looking southeast from top of Latting Observatory.* 1853 view by John Bachman. New-York Historical Society.

182(2)   *Crystal Palace. Section looking north, showing relationship with Croton Reservoir (right).* Drawing by Carstensen and Gildemeister, architects. Private collection.

183(3)   *Crystal Palace, interior view under dome. Inauguration ceremonies.* Engraving by F. Leslie from the *Illustrated News* of July 30, 1853. Author's collection.

183(4)   *"Crystal Palace Relics!"* Broadside poster. Museum of the City of New York.

184(1)   *Iron Pier, Coney Island, Brooklyn.* Stereoscope photograph. New-York Historical Society.

184(2)   *Iron Pier.* Stereoscope photograph. New-York Historical Society.

185(3)   *Iron Pier.* Stereoscope photograph. New-York Historical Society.

186(4)   *Recreation Pier.* From *The New Metropolis*, by E. Idell Zeisloft, 1899. Author's collection.

186(5)   *Kindergarten on Recreation Pier.* New York Public Library.

187(1)   *Steeplechase Park, Coney Island, Brooklyn. Looking north, and showing Parachute Jump (left).* Wide World Photos.

188(2)   *Steeplechase Park. Interior of main building.* 1910. Brooklyn Museum.

189(1)   *Dreamland, Coney Island, Brooklyn. "Roltair's Arabian Nights Up To Date."* Brooklyn Museum.

190(2)   *Dreamland. Main entrance.* Brooklyn Museum.

190(3)   *Dreamland. "The Dragons Gorge."* Brooklyn Museum.

191(1)   *Luna Park, Coney Island, Brooklyn. "Wormwoods Monkey Theatre."* Brooklyn Museum.

191(2)   *Luna Park, night view.* 1906. Samuel H. Gottscho.

192(1)   *World's Fair 1939, Flushing Meadow Park, Queens. National Cash Register Company building.* Museum of the City of New York.

231 (4)	*V-E Day, Times Square from Times Tower.* 1945. Bettmann/Corbis.
231 (5)	*V-E Day at night with brownout lifted, Times Square from Times Tower.* 1945. Bettmann/Corbis.
232 (6)	*New Year's Eve, Times Square.* 1950. Bettmann/Corbis.
232 (7)	*New Year's Eve, Times Square.* 2000. Nicole Bengivero/NYT Pictures.

DISASTERS

233	*Newspaper artist's drawing after police diagram of shooting of Stanford White by Harry K. Thaw, Roof Garden of Madison Square Garden, between Madison and Fourth Avenues, 26th and 27th Streets.* June 25, 1906. Bettmann/Corbis.
234 (1)	*Triangle Shirtwaist Company fire, Asch Building, northwest corner of Washington Place and Greene Street.* March 25, 1911. Bain. Author's collection.
234 (2)	*Former Triangle Shirtwaist (now New York University) building, northwest corner of Washington Place and Greene Street.* 1999. Nathan Silver.
235 (3)	*Coney Island fire.* July 1932. Culver Pictures.
235 (4)	*Ameko Kitchen Products building fire, Water Street.* July 1937. Weegee/ICP/Liaison Agency.
235 (5)	*La Guardia cartoon,* The New Yorker. Alain Brustlein, *The New Yorker*/Culver Pictures.
236 (1)	*The Half Moon Hotel, Coney Island.* Airmap Corporation of America.
237 (2)	*Police arrest of (seated, left to right) Harry "Pittsburgh" Strauss, Martin "Bugsy" Goldstein and Abe "Kid Twist" Reles, of Murder, Inc.* New York Daily News.
237 (3)	*The Half Moon Hotel, Coney Island, with Abe Reles's covered body on the lower roof.* November 1941. Bettmann/Corbis.
237 (4)	*Albert Anastasia's body being removed from the barbershop of the Park Sheraton Hotel, Seventh Avenue between 55th and 56th Streets.* October 25, 1957. Tom Baffer, *New York Daily News.*
238 (1)	*Borough President Julius Miller opening the Miller Elevated Highway (part of the West Side Highway).* November 1930. Joseph Costa, *New York Daily News.*
238 (2)	*The Normandie and the Queen Mary (camouflaged gray) in berths adjacent to the West Side Highway.* Hulton Getty/Liaison Agency.
238 (3)	*The Normandie burning at Pier 88.* February 9, 1942. Underwood & Underwood/Corbis.
239 (4)	*The Normandie capsized at Pier 88.* New York Daily News.
240 (1)	*The Empire State Building on fire after a plane crash. Smoke from lower roof is from part of the bomber wreckage.* July 28, 1945. Bettmann/Corbis.
241 (2)	*The Empire State Building impact collision, 78th and 79th floors. Part of bomber wreckage hangs from the 78th floor.* July 28, 1945. Bettmann/Corbis.

PLACES OF THE GREATS, THE CELEBRITIES, THE RIFF RAFF

242 (1)	*Arturo Toscanini and family.* Ca. 1910. Theater Collection, Museum of the City of New York.
242 (2)	*Enrico Caruso as the Duke in* Rigoletto. Ca. 1910. Theater Collection, Museum of the City of New York.
243 (3)	*Metropolitan Opera program for world premiere production of Puccini's* The Girl of the Golden West. December 10, 1910. Theater Collection, Museum of the City of New York.
243 (4)	*Curtain call of Maria Callas and Tito Gobbi at the old Met.* Bettmann/Corbis.
243 (5)	*The all-night queue waiting for the season's opening-night tickets at the old Met.* November 1949. Bettmann/Corbis.
244 (1)	*Columnist Walter Winchell and owner Sherman Billingsley at the Stork Club.* Culver Pictures.
244 (2)	*Ernest Hemingway and Martha Gellhorn at the Stork Club.* November 1940. Bettmann/Corbis.
244 (3)	*Marlene Dietrich and Jean Gabin at El Morocco.* Culver Pictures.
244 (4)	*The Stork Club, 3 East 53rd Street.* Bettmann/Corbis.
244 (5)	*Bar at the Stork Club.* October 1942. Bettmann/Corbis.
245 (6)	*El Morocco.* Florian de Narde. Theater Collection, Museum of the City of New York.
245 (7)	*Billy Rose's Diamond Horseshoe.* July 1940. Culver Pictures.
245 (8)	*The Latin Quarter.* Culver Pictures.
245 (9)	*The International Casino.* Culver Pictures.
246 (10)	*Frank Sinatra and Rocky Graziano chatting at the Copacabana.* April 1942. Bettmann/Corbis.
246 (11)	*Serviceman chatting with actress Olga San Juan at the Copacabana.* December 1942. Sonnee Gottlieb, Bettmann/Corbis.
246 (12)	*The Copacabana.* Florian de Narde. Theater Collection, Museum of the City of New York.
247 (13)	*Studio 54 interior at reopening.* September 25, 1979. Bettmann/Corbis.
247 (14)	*Studio 54 exterior.* January 1978. Bettmann/Corbis.
247 (15)	*Mineshaft exterior after closure by police.* Yvonne Hemsey/Liaison Agency.
247 (16)	*The Freely Box, Mineshaft.* Krasner/Trebitz/Liaison Agency.
247 (17)	*Plato's Retreat after reopening.* 1985. C. J. Zumwalt, *New York Daily News.*
247 (18)	*Plato's Retreat, notice board.* 1979. Bettmann/Corbis.

INDEX.

NOTE: Page numbers in italics refer to illustrations.

273